Informal Recreational Activities

Informal Recreation

American Camping Association
Bradford Woods
Martinsville, IN 46151

Activities: A Leader's Guide

By Dr. Phyllis M. Ford

Published 1977 by the American Camping Association
Bradford Woods
Martinsville, Indiana 46151

ⓒ Phyllis M. Ford 1974
First Edition Published 1974

Library of Congress Cataloging in Publication Data

Ford, Phyllis M
    Informal recreational activities.

    Bibliography: p.
    1. Recreation leadership.   I. Title.
GV181.4.F67   790'.02'02   77-22778
ISBN 0-87603-026-6

The cover photograph was taken by John D'Arcy, a day camp counselor for the YMCA of Omaha/Council Bluffs Metropolitan Area, IA. The campers pictured have participated in a backpack camp at YMCA Day Camp Pokamoke, IA.

Photos pages 6, 22, 52 courtesy of the Salvation Army, Pittsburgh, PA.

Photo page 95 courtesy of Bear Pole Ranch, Steamboat Springs, CO

Printed in the United States of America

Contents

Chapter 1
Leadership

There is no doubt that leadership ability is an enviable attribute and that leaders are always in great demand. This book is designed to be of help to people who find themselves in positions requiring face-to-face leadership with participants at playgrounds, social events, community centers, youth camps, or other similar situations.

The leadership materials presented here are a brief summary of many longer works and have been adapted to apply to the leader of recreational activities in informal settings. This is by no means a complete analysis of leadership. It is to be used for situations covered by the remaining chapters of this book.

LEADERSHIP DEFINED

The most commonly used definition of leadership found among recreation personnel appears to be that of Ordway Tead, who in his "Art of Leadership" writes that, "Leadership is the activity of influencing people to co-operate toward some goal which they come to find desirable."

This definition is really quite complete and all-encompassing. It explains that the leader not only motivates a group, but that he also spurs them into action toward some end which they may not have had in mind originally but which they eventually find desirable. An example of the great power of leadership as described by this definition is, of course, the ability of Adolf Hitler to motivate the German people to believe in and fight for Aryan Supremacy against the entire world. His motto, "Today Germany, tomorrow the World," became a national goal because of Hitler's leadership. This definition also explains that parental leadership can motivate a family to have fun cleaning out the garage.

A far less academic, but perhaps more appealing, definition of unknown origin states that, "A leader is a person with a magnet in his heart and a compass in his head." — a magnet to draw people to him and a compass to direct them in the right direction.

These definitions are good. They tell us something. They give us theories from which to work. Yet they do not analyze what makes recreation leaders tick. They do not explain how a playground, camp or youth leader can be successful. They start with the end product and describe it but do not mention the ingredients which go into making up the leader.

LEADERSHIP ANALYZED

When examining the many texts, articles or monographs on leadership, one finds that there are nine aspects of leadership generally agreed upon. There are three well-known ways in which one acquires a leadership position; three theories of what makes a person a leader; and three methods of leading. These overlap somewhat, but can be simplified as follows:

How do people acquire leadership positions?

1. They inherit the position. This is exemplified by the monarch who inherits his duties on the death of his father, or by the son whose father wills him the family business.
2. They are appointed. This is the way most people acquire positions of responsibility in leadership. Most persons appointed to leadership positions are appointed to relatively long-term positions and to positions having stated purposes and objectives. Leaders of recreation programs are generally appointed.
3. They emerge from the group itself. This leader is the one who is often unrecognized, yet who, because his work within the group and with the group, emerges from the group to stand out as the person to whom the group relates as a leader.

What are the theories of leadership?

1. The trait theory. This theory is based on the premise that a person must possess certain personal and social characteristics or traits in order to achieve leadership. This theory stresses personality as a major factor in leadership.
2. The situation theory. This theory maintains that different people become leaders as the situation demands. A person who takes over in an emergency and directs people out of a burning building may be an effective leader in that situation but not in other situations.
3. The group dynamics theory. This theory states that leadership is a group phenomenon with the leader leading through interaction with the group and its goals.

What are the three methods of leadership?

1. Autocratic or authoritarian. Here the leader dominates through power.

2. Democratic. The democratic leader shares, is people-oriented and is open-minded.
3. Laissez-faire. This method of leading may be an absence of leadership, for the group is allowed to set its own goals without restraints and to go its own way without guidance.

In summary then, we find nine commonly used terms related to leadership:

Inherited, Appointed and Emergent
Trait, Situation and Group Dynamics
Autocratic, Democratic and Laissez-faire

This is a gross over-simplification of the topic but it is quite an adequate and accurate capsulization of many lengthy works.

Generally it is stated that the democratic leader who emerges from the group as a result of a group dynamics is the most desirable leader. There are, however, situations wherein this leader would not get the job done. In the case of a highway accident, an autocratic, self-appointed leader who can react to the situation rapidly, cooly and wisely is the most desirable leader.

None of these above ideas or theories really states what it is which makes a leader successful. Nor do they examine why it is that some leaders are not successful when it would appear that they should be.

SOME DESIRABLE ATTRIBUTES

In spite of the fact that there is no concrete evidence that personality determines success, and that there is no definitely agreed upon list of traits which mark successful leaders, a list of ten recommended personal attributes is listed below. This list could be added to almost indefinitely, but the ten items presented here are among those frequently possessed by successful leaders of recreational events. They are not to be considered the only list of leadership traits nor are they always a winning combination. Still they are attributes for which a leader might strive in his progress to success.

Charisma Although the word charisma is very old, it is found only in quite modern dictionaries. It is a word which came into popularity during the lives of both John F. and Robert Kennedy. Charisma means, ''a divine power which draws people.'' Charisma is the magnet in the heart which draws people to the leader. Everyone has some power to draw people to him—not all of the people all of the time, but certainly, some of the people all the time, and all the people some of the time. This is product X. We cannot define it, but every leader must have some of this undefinable magnetic appeal.

Willingness Robert Frost said, ''The world is full of willing people; some willing to work, the others willing to let them.'' It is the person who is willing to work who has a chance to become a success.

Enthusiasm
.

We must qualify enthusiasm by saying that there are some enthusiastic people who remind us of the bottom half of the old fashioned double boiler. You know them; they are all steamed up but they don't have any idea what's cooking. We don't want that kind of enthusiasm in our recreation leaders. We do not want the enthusiastic leader who says, "Oh, it's a wonderful idea," but who does not really know how much work goes into it, how much time, how much cost, how much effort. We need enthusiastic leaders with some concrete knowledge behind their enthusiasm.

Initiative

Initiative is something which is individual. We may remember the story of the man who died and was visiting the "under world." He came upon a table that was piled high with the most sumptuous food imaginable. There was a long line of people on either side of the table. Both of these lines of people were starving to death, for on their wrists they had tied three-foot long spoons. They could not put the spoons into their food and then reach their mouths. The length from the elbow to the wrist is just long enough so that we can feed ourselves. With three-foot spoons on the end of our wrists, we can starve to death.

The man then visited the "Heavenly world," where he found a similar table piled high with sumptuous food. On either side of the table were laughing, happy, roly-poly, well-fed people. They too had spoons tied onto the ends of their wrists. But they were feeding each other. This is the kind of initiative that we need in our recreation leaders; initiative which enables us to help each other equally and mutually. We must have the initiative to overcome difficult situations successfully.

Standards

Abby Graham, an early YWCA worker has said, "It is important that we stand for something, or we'll fall for anything." Unfortunately we can find examples of a great many people in our society today who will fall for anything. We need to have ideals to reach for. Carl Schurz said, "Ideals are like stars, you will not succeed in touching them with your hands, but like sea-faring men on the desert of waters, you choose them as your guide and follow them to your destiny." We need ideals to reach for or we will never go far.

Industry

One cannot attain his ideals by dreaming about them. One has to work for them. It has been said that there are three and only three, important bones in the body: the wishbone, the jawbone and the backbone. Recreation leaders, working as hard as they do, know that the backbone is the important bone. That's the kind of industry that is needed.

Courage

A Harvard philosopher used to take his vacation out in the mountains of the west. And daily, because he did not ride horseback, he would walk. One day coming back from one of his walks, an old-timer said to him, "Well, professor where have you been?"

"Just out for a walk," said the professor.

"You'd better watch out," said the old-timer, "you're apt to get lost."

"No," said the professor, "I have never been lost in my life."

"Well, said the old-timer, "out here, anybody who ain't never been lost, ain't never been very far."

And then the professor realized that he needed to go further; he needed to have the courage to get lost. Our leaders need the courage to try new things, to try new ways, to do better even though they are not successful at first. They need to have the courage to work for their ideals.

Pride

There are a great many important, wise people in the world and many of us would like to be important, wise or famous. We think that what we are doing may not really amount to anything. Leaders need to develop some knowledge and some skills and be proud of the humble abilities they have.

A poem by Elizabeth Thomas goes:
"Once upon a time, I planned to be
An artist or celebrity.
A song I thought to write some day
And all the world would homage pay.
I longed to write a noted book
But what I did was learn to cook.
For life with simple tasks is filled,
And I have not done what I willed.
Yet when I see boys' hungry eyes,
I'm glad I make good apple pies."

That's the kind of pride we need in our leaders.

Optimism

This is a pessimistic world. We are told that by the year 2000 the world may come to an end. We are told we are over-populated and over-polluted. A great many of our young people today have a defeatist attitude about those problems. They are pessimists. The difference between the pessimist and the optimist is that an optimist gets up in the morning, goes to the window, opens the draperies, looks out and says, "Good morning, Lord." A pessimist gets up in the morning, crawls to the window, peeks through the draperies, and says, "Good Lord,—Morning!" We want leaders to be like the optimist—all day, every day!

Giving

There is an old Italian proverb which says, "What you keep, you lose. What you give away is yours forever." We may know how to make apple pies, but we will lose that ability if we don't make the pies and give them to somebody. We may know how to sing and lead singing, but we will lose that if we don't sing and lead singing. We know how to laugh but we will lose it if we don't share our joy and laugh with others. Every attribute that a person has becomes strengthened as he uses it, as he gives it to others. This quality is very important in our leaders, for it not only may determine their success as leaders, but it may also determine their success as human beings.

ADVICE

The leader may make a list of other attributes he feels help him to lead. Perhaps he would prefer to use the following four items as his guides.

Be a Real Person This means exactly what it says. There is no place in recreation for a "phoney," for one who is insincere, or for one who is ego-centric, selfish, or disinterested. A real person has a genuine sincerity and a positive outlook.

Like People Most people admit to liking others. They do not always realize what this means. Often, when people say they like other people, they inadvertently think of people who are like themselves or like their friends. A recreation leader, or any leader, must like all people: young, old; obese, undernourished; handsome, unattractive; noisy, quiet; happy, discouraged; affluent, destitute; bright, dull; good-natured, grouchy; polished, uncouth; and more. The leader must like people for what they are as individuals and for what they may become as individuals. He should not like people only as they relate to him and his standards, but he should like them as they relate to their potential.

Know Job In other words plan, prepare, study, practice, and keep up to date. Don't try to work "off the top of your head." A good leader is a prepared leader.

Have Fun If you don't enjoy leading, you may not be cut out for a leadership position. Certainly a good leader enjoys his job and there is more in recreation positions to be enjoyed than there is in many other positions.

There is no doubt that leadership is work. Successful supervision of situations in which participants need specific directions takes considerable planning based on acquired knowledge. The remaining chapters in this book are designed to help the recreation leader plan for events which are not generally covered in depth in the readily available text books.

The journey of a thousand miles begins with a single step."
—Lao Tse.

Chapter 2
Preliminary Considerations in Leading

The art of leading well appears, on the surface, to be a spontaneous action occurring between the leader and the participants. This apparent ease is rather unfortunate at times because it induces some people to try to be playground, community center or camp leaders without realizing that much of the actual work involved in leadership occurs in the preparation.

BASIC STEPS

Objectives The first step in leading any single activity or series of activities is to understand the fundamental objectives of play leadership. We hear much concerning objectives today, often with little understanding of the meaning of the word or of its significance. Simply defined, a set of objectives is really a list of things which we hope to accomplish through a specific activity. Objectives should be attainable; consequently, the things we hope to accomplish should actually be within the sphere of each participant's ability. Regardless of objectives for each individual activity, the general or all-encompassing objectives for recreation programs are:
1. To provide for the enjoyment of the participants,
2. To present activities which are both wholesome and safe,
3. To teach the skills necessary for successful participation in activities.

It is easy to understand the first objective, for unless an activity is enjoyable or evokes pleasure, it can not be termed recreation. Sometimes during the learning process an activity is not particularly pleasurable; however, if enjoyment is eventually forthcoming, the objective has been attained. But since the activities and participants always differ greatly in their respective make-ups, the leader is constantly challenged to find a wide variety of activities so that each participant experiences true enjoyment.

Presenting wholesome and safe activities relates to the selection of activities which are wholesome not only physically, but also socially, psychologically, and emotionally. Leaders must be especially careful that no activity ridicules or embarrasses anyone. All activities must be of a quality which uplifts, not downgrades. Poor or mediocre quality which occasionally results from indiscriminate selection of activities can never be justified.

Many recreation leaders feel that the teaching of skills related to activities is of inconsequential importance because recreation is fundamentally concerned with enjoyment. Practicing skills is often not enjoyable they feel. This argument is far from sound; teaching no skills or condoning incorrect skill execution actually does the participant a disservice. The better the skills, the higher the quality of enjoyment. The tennis player who has never been taught how to serve correctly never becomes a real tennis player. The girl who is allowed to throw a ball without making use of the laws of follow-through and opposition will soon realize she doesn't know how to throw and will lose interest. The child who cuts himself with a new jack knife because no one taught him safety has not received full benefit of leadership.

Beyond these three fundamental recreation-oriented objectives, each activity is led with additional objectives in mind. Keeping the three fundamental objectives in mind, the leader can move on to planning his program.

Facility Analysis

An early preparatory consideration for recreation leading is the study of the facility or area where the activities are to take place. Prior to using an indoor facility for the first time, the activity director should examine the room or building to learn as much about it as possible. Where are all the exits? How is the heat controlled? Do the windows open? How are the lights controlled? Are there rest rooms for men and for women? Where? Are there any kitchen facilities? What kinds of refreshments can be served? Where are the electrical outlets? What about fire escapes? Drinking fountains? Waste baskets? What is in the closets? Where is the closest telephone?

Whenever the leader plans to direct active games and contests indoors, it is imperative that he determine what he will use for boundaries and goals. Many recreation areas have floor lines which, while initially intended for something else, may be adapted for informal games and relays. If a leader decides he must put lines on the floor he should never use chalk; chalk has an abrasive quality which leaves the mark of the line on the finish of the floor even after the color and chalk dust have been removed.

Masking tape appears to be the most acceptable temporary floor marking today. Unlike plastic adhesive tape it is easily removed; however, when lines are to remain for any duration, the colored plastic tapes are best. On washable floors, longer lasting and easily removed lines may be applied with water colors which will wash off with plain water. For a short time, however, masking tape seems to be the best material to use for floor markings.

If the playing area is a city park or playground, the leader should make a complete tour every time he uses it. He needs to be familiar with all of the playing courts and equipment on his first visit. On subsequent visits he needs to check equipment for splinters, breaks, loose bolts, etc. He must constantly be on the alert for broken glass, cans, bottles and other debris. He also needs to check the same types of facilities he looked for in the indoor area. Knowledge of the locations of restrooms, drinking fountains, telephones, waste containers and equipment storage areas is just as important outdoors as indoors.

Needs of Participants Every activity in a program must be selected only after careful consideration of several points, the first of which is consideration of the participant. Unless one has an understanding of the age and sex characteristics of the participants accompanied by an analysis of the proposed activity, one has no rationale for selecting a recreational event. Besides general age and sex characteristics, one must keep in mind the group's purpose for attending the events, special factors (such as handicaps, long-time friends, strangers, frequency of attendance) and the expectations of the group.

Activity Analysis Each type of recreation program—playground, campfire, party, song fest, or other—has its own format which determines the type of activities to be included and the order in which they should be presented. Before actually planning any one specific program the leader should be familiar with its objectives, structure and components. Only then has he any knowledge of what kinds of activities are to be considered. Special kinds of programs are discussed in subsequent sections.

Activities must be carefully analyzed to determine whether or not the action is suitable for the group and to assure a variety of action. It is here that the ability to classify is needed. Also one must not overlook the equipment needed, the space required, and the time which must be allotted. Many activities, otherwise quite acceptable, must be eliminated from plans if they are too complicated for the group, too time-consuming, involve unavailable equipment or take up too much space.

Whenever an activity is considered desirable but not practical, effort should be made to adapt it to the situation. Ability to change, modify and adapt rules, equipment, playing area, and skills is a desirable trait found in far too few leaders.

Each activity proposed should be subjected to the following analysis:

1. What movement does the activity entail? What skills?
2. What form does the activity take?
3. What are the psychological attributes of the activity?

4. How does this differ from other activities in the program?
5. How is it similiar?
6. How can the activity be presented so it is wholesome and safe?
7. What are the objectives for presenting this activity? What do I hope this activity will do to and for the participant?

In this manner, a leader can answer readily any questions concerning why any activity was included in the program. No activity should be led for the specific reason of filling time, killing time or keeping busy!

Preparation   To run smoothly, the program requires leaders who know their material thoroughly. There is no place for note cards stuck in pockets to be brought forth either blatantly or stealthily to find out what comes next. It may be permissible to make notes on the sequence of activities in a program but to read directions for a skill, or words to a song, or to look up the rules to an activity says to the participant, "You really were not important enough for me to prepare thoroughly." Further, the participant soon equates leadership with the reading of directions.

While the activities are being planned, attention must be paid to details of equipment. Not only must it be prepared in advance, but allowance should be made for the unexpected need for extras and for breakage. Plans must also be made for retrieving equipment following an activity. It is amazing how many leaders will go on to a new activity or turn the program over to an associate for a new activity without arranging to really complete the previous activity by cleaning up. Certain types of equipment left lying around can be the cause of tripping accidents, and any unused material is unsightly and detracts from the present activity.

A final word of advice in early preparation is: over-plan. It is far better to plan five extra activities and not use them than to plan five too few and wonder how to fill up the time. Suggestions from the participants may be good in many situations but often are not in keeping with the theme, take too long to explain, require difficult skills or equipment and in general detract from the continuity of a pre-planned program.

Attitude   While it may seem to be an obvious point, the attitude of the leader is worthy of mention. As in no other occupation, the recreation leader must be pleasant. This does not necessitate that he become the gushing over-exuberant, eager patronizer whose popularity is as fleeting as the sincerity of his smile. It does, however, necessitate showing warmth, good nature, interest, enthusiasm and honest concern for the welfare of the participants in spite of fatigue, colds, headache, inadequate facilities, poor equipment or other distracting elements. In his preparation, the leader must realize that while he is not personally interested in leading ten-year old activities for the 15th time, the important concern is not the activities, but the ten-year-olds who are reached through the activities.

SAFETY FACTORS

No matter what the activity is or where the event occurs, the leader's prime responsibility is really the welfare of the participants. In active events particularly, certain isolated considerations are worthy of mention.

Boundaries What boundaries to use always seems to be an early question in the preparation for leading low organized games and contests. The most obvious and logical appearing boundaries are often the most dangerous and impractical. Walls, fences, trees and sidewalks bordering grassy fields are poor boundaries when used for goals, turning points or end lines. Children running to be "safe" from a tagger will run as fast as they can until stopped by the immobile wall. A child who puts out his hands to stop his impact can break his wrists if his weight hits at the wrong angle. A child who trips just before reaching the wall cannot protect his head. The author once witnessed a child fall into a wall boundary and break her glasses. The resulting cut above the eye required six stitches. Children using a wall to mark the end of a race will often throw themselves headlong into the wall in order to reach it sooner. The "It," in his eagerness to tag a runner who has nearly reached the wall, may fall forward and push the runner into this stationary boundary. Furthermore, the hard abrasive quality of a sidewalk is of too much contrast to the softer, usually slippery, surface of a grassy area. A child trying to avoid tagging often leaps right past the sidewalk and into the street.

Better boundaries or goals may be comprised of areas marked off several feet from the wall or fence. In a gymnasium, many possibilities exist for marking areas as wide as the playing court and as deep as five or ten feet. There are times when the far end of the goal area must be close to the wall or the wall itself. When that is the case, runners can be admonished that they are "safe" when inside the goal area, but will be considered "caught" if they touch the wall.

Indoor goals are best marked either permanently or by masking tape; although, movable markers like those outside may be substituted. Number ten cans filled with sand, or corrugated cartons and sand, are good. Old towels or sweat shirts are good outside but are hazards inside, since they slip on the smooth surface of the floor when stepped on.

Many times turf playgrounds have no lines for goals and the leader must use a trail of a material known as "dry line" which is not harmful to the skin or eyes. This is a substance used widely for playground markings. A row of objects spaced five to ten feet apart may also be used as markers. Burlap bags partly filled with sand or sawdust or onion sacks filled with foam rubber are very practical. Ropes pegged down are very dangerous and should never be permitted; nasty trips and falls can occur even if the youngsters are warned to be careful.

Footwear   When running occurs indoors, it is the recommended practice for all participants to wear tennis shoes or sneakers. Generally every leader takes only a short time to notice incorrect footwear and request that the incorrectly shod children remove their shoes. But this practice, while saving the floor, creates a hazard because the children slide in their socks and lose control of speed, direction and pivoting, and consequently often fall. It is far better to have them remove their socks and play in bare feet than to slide around in stockings risking cracked skulls.

Circle   Several running activities require that the participants
Activities sit in a circle, facing toward the center.

1. Position. An accepted position is with the legs stretched out in front, and the weight leaning back on the arms which are stretched out in back, fingers pointed outward. However, in this comfortable position, the participant risks getting his fingers trampled by runners on the outside of the circle. A better position is "Indian Style," crosslegged with hands on or near the ankles.

2. Direction. For consistency and security, youngsters need to feel that they will do something correct in each activity. If the direction of travel for circle activities is consistently counter-clockwise, the very young child will feel somewhat at home, even with new variations. If he doesn't have to worry about where he is going each time, he can concentrate on what he is to do. Therefore, whenever the circle moves or someone chases another player, the action should always be counter-clockwise. The reason behind this accepted pattern is unknown, but it is the direction followed in folk, square and couple dances, in track meets, in auto and horse racing, and in countless other sports. In some activities, one person runs counter-clockwise and the others run clockwise.

3. Meeting someone who is going in the opposite direction. Often those running around the circle go in opposite directions and young children have a tendency to meet head on when not cautioned otherwise. Telling them to pass on the right may be confusing; yet nearly all of them will understand which way to to if told to pretend they are driving a car and to stay on the same side of the road on which their parents drive. Having them touch hands as they pass is often too involved for an excited four or five-year-old; they either miss and have to retract steps, slap too hard, or grab hold and forget to let go when their opponent has passed them.

Tagging   To an adult, tagging is a simple matter requiring no discussion, but to a four or five-year-old, tagging may be a new skill. It is important that children learn that tagging is merely touching someone on the back, arm or shoulder. While the leader never mentions that tagging is not pushing or slapping (Why give children ideas for action which you wish to prevent?), he must be on the lookout for the child who "forgets" how to touch.

Of equal importance is teaching the child to admit he is tagged. Here is the beginning of basic sportsmanship. Here a child learns to recognize the success of another and his own failure. Here he learns that the penalty for being caught in a game situation is of minor consequence and there is no shame to it. But this is a learned reaction, actually quite contradictory to the egocentric nature of a four or five-year-old. The sportsmanship of the player later on in team sports starts its development in the simple tagging activities of low organization played by pre-schoolers. One can not deny the necessity for this early application of the fundamentals of sportsmanship.

Blindfolds
In the activities requiring successive children to be blind-folded, it is wise to protect the eyes from possible contagious infection and dirt passed from child to child as the blind-fold is shared. Simple protection is acquired through the use of individual facial tissues folded and placed over the eyes before affixing the blind-fold.

Ending Activities
It is a wise recreation leader who knows when to stop one activity and lead into another one; there is no way to predict when is the most expeditious moment. One slogan among many leaders is "Kill it before it dies," which means, stop the activity before anyone is tired of it. When this moment may be is an unfathomable question, yet the moment after boredom sets in may be easy to see. The leader must try to have everyone have an enjoyable experience. It is far better to receive groans for stopping an event than groans for continuing an activity in which there is no interest.

Still a leader must not stop an activity too soon. There must be ample time to build up an interest, to take several turns and to give everyone a chance for some type of enjoyable participation. A new activity which is fairly complicated may need to be stopped early because it is still new and not a favorite; yet stopping it too soon prevents anyone from having a chance to develop an interest in it. "Kill it before it dies" is a wise slogan. Finding the best moment comes only through constant experience, knowledge of the activity, and, above all, a kinship of feeling with and for the participant.

GETTING PARTICIPATION

Not everyone wants to participate all the time. Some want to participate and don't know how to join in. A sensitive leader must notice the late-comer, the stand-off ones, the hesitators, the on-lookers, the sour grape types,

and assume that some of them really do want to participate and only need encouragement.

One way to get non-participants into the act is to ask
them to join the group. Some people will respond when
assured that the group needs them. They may realize they
are needed to fill positions, even up the teams, or just be
of help by being part of the group.

With the very young, putting out a hand works well, as
they often reach for the outstretched hand and allow themselves to be led into the action. But beware of this with
children over eight, many of whom feel that only babies
hold hands. Sometimes people really do not want to
participate and should be allowed to watch rather than be
forced into an unpleasant situation. Don't assume,
however, that they will never want to participate. Give
them occasional quiet recognition and ask again if they
would like to join in.

CORRECTING ERRORS

No one is perfect and no matter how carefully the
instructions are given errors will occur. Handling errors
tactfully is a skill to be cultivated carefully and, regardless
of the kind of error, kindness is always the password.
There are times when it is advisable to blame errors on
your own weakness or poor teaching techniques.
Naturally, the best time for this is when the fault really
does lie with leadership errors. Children love to find a
leader who is so human he makes errors. It puts the leader
closer to their level. Adults, too, find that occasional
errors on the part of the leader refreshing. Sometimes,
when an activity is complicated, it raises the morale of
struggling participants if the leader can pleasantly admit
to going too fast or getting too involved.

Usually it is possible to make a quick analysis of the
reason for any errors. It is usually found that errors were
made because skills were incorrectly or inadequately
taught.

ELIMINATION GAMES

An elimination game is one in which the object is to
eliminate the players one by one until only one individual
remains. This definition tells us that elimination games
violate the initial spirit of recreation, for any activity which
aims to cut down on participants hardly contributes to the
goal of participation for all. Most elimination games, such
as dodge ball, find the most highly skilled player getting
the most practice, as he stays in the game the longest,
while the one who needs the practice the most is
eliminated first.

In some cases, and with players of fairly equal ability,
elimination type games have great merit. They inspire
effort; they promote competition; they contribute to

sportsmanship; and they actually enhance skills. On the other hand, when players are inexperienced, unskilled, or of unequal ability, elimination type games create discouragement or embarrassment and those eliminated lose interest. The problem of what to do with those eliminated may always plague the leader unless there is enough equipment to continuously form new games with the eliminated, an endless process.

Most elimination games can be modified so that, instead of being eliminated, the players are allowed to continue. Dodge ball has half-a-dozen modifications. Some games move those making errors to new positions. Some give each errant player a letter to spell out GHOST, HORSE or DOG. When one player has spelled out the designated word the game is over or started again.

MISCELLANEOUS

A few additional, brief comments may help the beginning leader appear experienced. Participate when it is practical, but don't try to play and judge at the same time. Pace the activities so vigorous ones are interspersed with quiet ones. And whenever possible, shift the leadership. Let the participants take over. They'll love it!

> *"Children need models more than they need critics."*
> — Joseph Joubert

Chapter 3
Basic Guides for Activity Leadership

Any recreation leader who finds himself leading a variety of activity programs continuously, soon develops a set of steps which he comes to follow automatically with consistently successful results. While there are specific guidelines for specific programs, the following material is basic to leadership of any activity:
1) Get the attention of the group.
2) Arouse interest.
3) Direct the group into the formation for the activity.
4) Give directions

EXPLANATION OF STEPS

While knowing these four steps is important, they alone will not guarantee success and need a considerable amount of explanation to be fully understood.

Getting Attention

Several means of getting attention are recognized as having effectiveness in different situations. Probably the "attention getter" which comes to mind most frequently is the shrill blast of a referee's whistle. The whistle is indeed an excellent attention device if used with restraint. The advantage of a whistle is the ease with which it can be heard in a large area such as a playfield or a gymnasium. For this reason, a whistle should not be used in the confines of a small room, or with a small group standing in close proximity to the leader. Over-use of the whistle soon results in a complete lack of attention to it. The leader who blows the whistle for continual random announcements displays a gross lack of organization. The leader who uses a whistle well, conditions his group to stop activity and listen when they hear one long, sharp blast. The whistle must be blown with vigor and the sound should end sharply and not be drawn out.

In small areas, or with smaller groups, other noise-makers can suffice to arouse attention. A bell, a horn, a buzzer, a popped balloon, the beating of a tom-tom, the clapping of hands, or countless other sounds will attract attention. Pre-schoolers are often trained to respond to chords played on the piano by stopping their free-play and stationing themselves in certain areas in anticipation of a new activity.

Attention also may be gained without the use of noise. In a building, the flashing of the lights will often be used. Pre-school children soon can learn that if the leader stands in a specific spot it means time for a surprise, a story, a new game, or a song. (And what fun it is to catch the leader on "the spot" quite by accident and unprepared for any surprise!)

An attention signal used almost universally in summer camps and among youth-serving agencies is the raised hand. The historical background of the raised hand tells us that when Indians travelled single file through the forest, the leader signalled his followers when to stop and be silent by raising his hand palm forward, to the height of his head. Each person on down the line followed suit; thus the entire line was stopped without the raising of even a whisper.

The recreational hand sign for silence is similar in that the leader stands silently with raised hand. Each person seeing the leader's hand, or that of another person standing in the same manner, does the same until the entire room is made up of silent, hand-raised individuals waiting to hear what comes next.

It often takes several minutes to quiet a group down in this manner and on the first few trials it is usually necessary to remind people that the raised hand means a quiet tongue even though a conversation is incomplete. Patience and pleasantness on the part of the leader will soon pay off in a group conditioned to paying attention to the hand signal which certainly is an impressive means of getting attention in a dining hall, campfire circle or meeting room.

Use of the human voice may be good for arousing attention IF the voice is well modulated and toned for attention. A low voice, with words spoken slowly is effective where a high, nasal voice is ignored. Many leaders find it necessary to practice projecting their voices across a sea of faces so that the tones and words are picked up easily by the group farthest away.

Once attention has been aroused, it must be kept by talking to the entire group at once. Lengthy directions, talking down to any audience, and a voice which is either too soft or too strident will lose attention as fast as it was gained.

Too often the leaders talk to groups before getting their attention. To be sure that everyone in the audience is listening takes practice and awareness of the individuals in the group. Often just waiting patiently and silently will help get the attention of the last few talkers.

Position   A key to gaining and keeping group attention is to stand where you can be seen and heard by all. Because the position of the group members changes, the leader must be constantly aware of his own position and place himself advantageously as the following figures indicate.

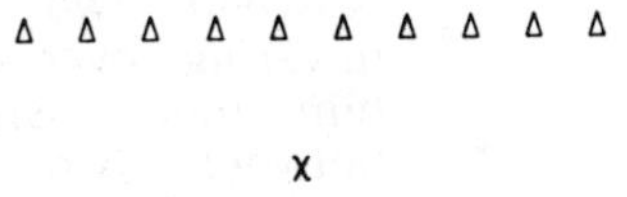

Δ Δ Δ Δ Δ Δ Δ Δ Δ Δ

X

FIGURE 1. When Working with a Single Line.
Note: Leader is positioned equidistant from each end, thus not giving one end less attention than the other.

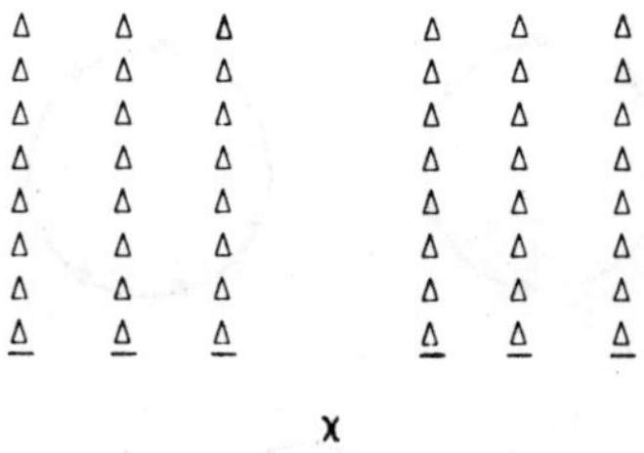

```
Δ    Δ    Δ          Δ    Δ    Δ
Δ    Δ    Δ          Δ    Δ    Δ
Δ    Δ    Δ          Δ    Δ    Δ
Δ    Δ    Δ          Δ    Δ    Δ
Δ    Δ    Δ          Δ    Δ    Δ
Δ    Δ    Δ          Δ    Δ    Δ
Δ    Δ    Δ          Δ    Δ    Δ
Δ    Δ    Δ          Δ    Δ    Δ
```
X

FIGURE 2. Working with an Even Number of Files.
Note: Leader is positioned in front of space dividing files in two. Center aisle space is a little larger than space between other lines.
No participant should be blocked from the leader's view by another participant.

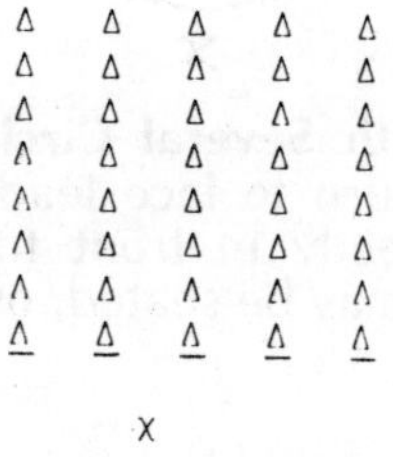

```
Δ    Δ    Δ    Δ    Δ
Δ    Δ    Δ    Δ    Δ
Δ    Δ    Δ    Δ    Δ
Δ    Δ    Δ    Δ    Δ
Δ    Δ    Δ    Δ    Δ
Δ    Δ    Δ    Δ    Δ
Δ    Δ    Δ    Δ    Δ
Δ    Δ    Δ    Δ    Δ
```
X

FIGURE 3. Working with an Uneven Number of Files.
Note: In this case, leader is NOT centered because standing in front of the center file would obstruct his view of all center file participants behind the first one.

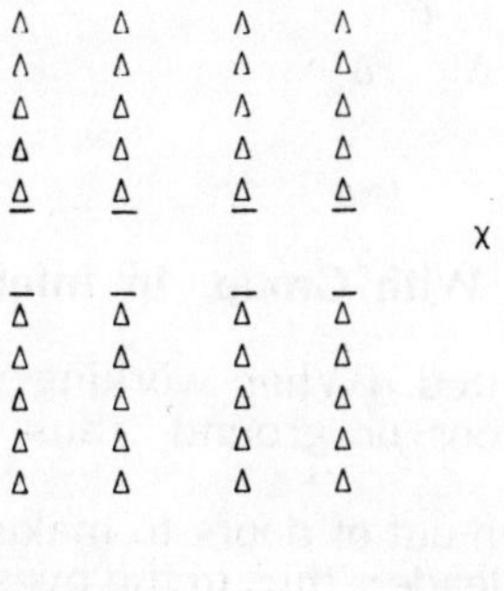

```
Λ    Λ    Λ    Λ
Λ    Λ    Λ    Δ
Δ    Δ    Λ    Δ
Δ    Δ    Δ    Δ
Δ    Δ    Δ    Δ
```
X

FIGURE 4. Working with Shuttle Relay Formation.

```
Δ    Δ    Δ    Δ
Δ    Δ    Δ    Δ
Δ    Δ    Δ    Δ
Δ    Δ    Δ    Δ
Δ    Δ    Δ    Δ
```

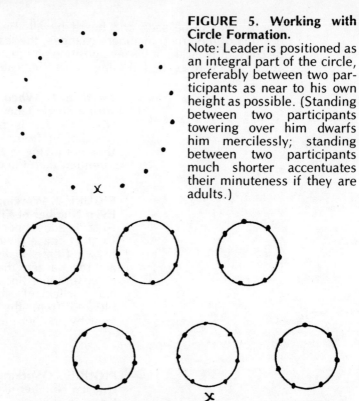

FIGURE 5. Working with Circle Formation.
Note: Leader is positioned as an integral part of the circle, preferably between two participants as near to his own height as possible. (Standing between two participants towering over him dwarfs him mercilessly; standing between two participants much shorter accentuates their minuteness if they are adults.)

FIGURE 6. Working with Several Circles [or Squares].
Note: Circle members turn to face leader who explains action, using circle directly in front to demonstrate if necessary. Participants may be seated, or leader elevated for better control.

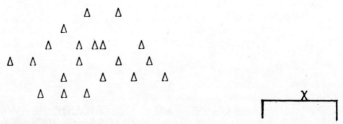

FIGURE 7. Working With Group. In Informal or Mass Formation.
Note: Leader is elevated. (When working with children, seat them on the floor or ground, thus elevating the leader.)
Caution must be taken out of doors to make sure that the sun is not behind the leader, thus in the eyes of the group. The leader should face into the sun, and wear sunglasses to keep him from squinting.

The elevated leader facing the sun is far better off than the leader who forces his group to look up at him and into the sun. Any speaker working indoors should be careful not to position himself between his audience and an undraped window unless he wishes to appear as a black silhouette against a brilliant streak of light, thus blinding the group and forcing the focus away from him.

Arousing Interest

In directing recreational activities, one hopes that the participants will participate with enthusiasm. Consequently, the leader develops the ability to motivate interest through unique introductions to the activities. Announcing the name of the next activity is poor methodology for several reasons. In the first place, it is a dogmatic, authoritarian leader who announces, "Now we are going to play . . . " Not only does this antagonize some people, but it also divides the group attention into several foci, some of which may be:

1) Good, I like that.
2) Oh, dear, I prefer something else.
3) Too bad, I don't know how to do it.
4) I wonder if he knows the rules our last leader knew.

In order to maintain even attention and order, and to arouse interest and curiosity, it is best not to announce an activity by title. An activity can be given a build-up according to the season, the weather, the theme of the parts or recent current events. At Christmas, the Calf Roping Relay (See Appendix) becomes the Christmas Gift Tying Relay; at Halloween, it becomes the Spider's Web. But at no time is it introduced as the String Wrapping Relay.

The purpose of the unique introduction is defeated if one starts with a question, "How would you like to . . . ?" for immediately control is lost as the group members reply, "Yes," "No," "Goodie," "Yeah," "Ugh," "Never," or whatever comes to their minds. Sometimes interest is aroused simply by the leader manipulating a piece of equipment to be used in the activity, particularly if it is a new activity. The best way to arouse interest in string activities is purely through forming unique string figures. This serves as an attention getter, interest arouser and grouping device all in one as curious spectators crowd around to see what is going on.

The same is true of the Eskimo or Indian yo-yo, that curious device which consists of a three or four foot piece of twine on each end of which is a round ball, horse chestnut or wooden sphere. The leader holds the line just off center, sends one sphere clockwise as he holds the other stationary, then suddenly sends the second sphere counter-clockwise and keeps them in momentum with a slight vertical hand motion. Soon everyone wants to do it, or try it and a craft session is born, out of which comes a yo-yo tournament. Instant attention, interest, grouping, and program!

Granted, it is not easy to think of things to say to introduce activities but with initiative and practice each leader can develop his own inimitable style.

Group Formation

Both children and adults can understand directions and patterns of movement better if they are positioned where they can visualize the patterns and act them out vicariously as directions are given. It is important, therefore, to position a group in as near game formation as possible before giving directions. Actually, the less moving of participants from one position to another the better.

An excellent reference for several methods of groupings is found in "Social Games for Recreation" by Evelyn Borst and Elmer D. Mitchell (Ronald Press, New York.)

Choosing The "It"

It is ironic that, in spite of the fact that the object of many activities of low organization is to keep from becoming, "It," most children want to start the game in that position. This is a good indication of the egocentricity of children aged four to eight, the very children who participate most in low organized games. It should be obvious, then, that a wise leader rarely asks who wants to be "It"; at least he doesn't unless he is prepared to make a choice of his own among the group's 25 to 50 per cent who plead, "Let me!" "Let me," "No. ME!" Asking for volunteers then, is not an efficient technique, but there is a good activity which eliminates all but one of the volunteers. The activity, Horsengoggle, (See Appendix) is also good for selecting the one of many who want a left-over piece of cake!

Choosing a youngster arbitrarily is the fastest yet most autocratic method; while asking youngsters to select their own "It" is often the slowest and most democratic method. It may be that the "It" chosen by the group is the most popular youngster and one who receives more than his share of attention.

With younger children, the leader can be autocratic in a surreptitious way by asking for an "It" in red tennis shoes, or someone wearing new jeans, or someone who just returned from a vacation. If the leader is observant, he can give recognition to those who seem to be lacking any, thus turning his arbitrary selection into a healthy one. Older children will, of course, see through the surreptitious request for "an 'It' wearing a yellow hair ribbon." They will prefer an arbitrary request such as, "Tom, will you be 'It' next?" as long as someone different is chosen each time and the someone is likely to play his role fairly and actually try to stop being "It" as soon as possible.

Some youngsters, enjoying being the center of attraction will make no attempt to cease being the "It" and will stay in the center of the circle until the leader gives him the warning, "One more try, Henry, and then we'll have to pick a new 'It.'" This technique usually results in some fast activity on "It's" part!

LEADING BASIC GAMES

Activities of different types require either slightly modified or additional techniques for successful leadership. The position of the players, the kinds of equipment, and the objectives of the activity all determine the methodology for teaching different events.

Low Organization Games
Simple games are of extreme seriousness to the young participant. But they may seem so simple to the leader that he over-simplifies his directions and the child gets "lost." A common error among leaders is to give too many directions at once, rather than to break the activity into parts. The child who says, "I don't get it," probably can't visualize what he is to do and probably has stopped listening as soon as he realizes this.

Of course the first thing the leader must do is to examine the activity thoroughly so that he understands the basic skills involved, the objective of the game, the playing area, the player positions, the rules, and the penalties for violation. Naturally, in introducing the game he follows the basic rules:

1) Get attention
2) Arouse interest
3) Place the players in a formation as close to the game situation as possible

The next step is to introduce the activity and its equipment if there is any. Do not pass equipment out; just introduce it. Since games of low organization are for young children with short attention spans. Handing out equipment will focus all attention on the equipment and none on the skill. Actually, most games of low organization use no equipment.

The next step is the explanation of the skill involved. If it is a new skill, it must be explained fully. Tagging, jumping, dodging, pivoting, throwing, hopping, catching, must be taught and practiced. Either the leader can demonstrate simple skills or have a participant help by demonstrating.

Then the players can practice the new skill without the equipment. For example, the activity known as Call Ball requires a player to throw a playground ball up in the air as he calls a name. Children need to practice with an imaginary ball so that they learn to use their legs, hold the ball correctly, start the ball low, and most important, follow through "to the sky." If they don't all practice the throw and follow through to the sky, each beginner in his turn will toss the ball straight across the circle. After they have practiced the toss they need to practice the catch. "Reach out, hold the ball, bring it in to you." These verbal cues will aid a vicarious experience and help develop the skill.

The leader needs to have children practice hopping so they use their ankles, knees and hips as springs. They need to practice to see how quietly they can hop, jump, run, or skip. The beginner needs to pretend to tag so that he learns to "touch," not push.

Children really want to know what they are going to do. The rules are only the ways the skills are used and of no meaning to a child unless he has a need for them. If he understands the action, the child is receptive to the rules. And through the vicarious experience of practice without equipment, he can already feel secure in his chances for success.

Then the game itself may be explained. It is best to divide it into parts and teach one part at a time or use a few players to demonstrate. There are no specific guides for when or how to divide a game of low organization into parts. This is up to the initiative of each individual leader. Actually, teaching games of low organization is the same as teaching a highly developed team sport: skills, drills, rules and playing. Unfortunately, the leader often forgets that a game of low organization may be as highly complicated to a seven-year-old as baseball is to a fourteen-year-old.

All this explanation of skills and rules should never take more than five minutes for games of low organization. The rules are few and simple; the attention span is short. It is better to start play and interrupt it for further rule explanation than to keep children standing around while the talk goes on and on. During the play, the leader must allow for individual differences since some children will learn must faster than others. There are times when slight errors may be over-looked in order to keep continuity in the activity and not embarrass an individual.

Of course, the leader should remember "kill it before it dies," and be sure to reveal the name of the game somewhere so that the children will know what to call it if they wish to request it or discuss it.

In summary, then, the steps for low organized activities are:

1. Examine the activity thoroughly
2. Get attention
3. Arouse interest
4. Group participants into a formation as close to game situation as possible
5. Explain the skill
6. Practice the skill without equipment
7. Explain some of the rules
8. Start play, stop occasionally to add more rules
9. "Kill it before it dies"

High Organization Games

Games of higher organization should follow the same basic steps as low organized games except that the players should be allowed to practice the skill with the equipment before the rules are given. Games such as Tetherball, Four-Square and Sidewalk Tennis are best taught by having a few participants learn the skills, practice the skills, learn a few simple rules involving the start of the game, execute the skills and play the game while the others listen and watch. Many times a leader and one or more participants demonstrating the game is far more efficient than a lecture. Rule infractions may be explained as they occur, thus giving onlookers visual pictures of situations.

Scoring may not be taught for several days in such things as Table Tennis, Hand Tennis, etc. Actually, the beginner is far more interested in performing the skill than in checking the score; in many recreational situations keeping score is of minor significance. Certainly, though, learning how to score correlates highly with learning advanced skills. In all cases, correct skill execution should be emphasized.

Table Games

Table games are best taught by a leader and one or more volunteer opponents who sit at the table in playing position with the others gathered around so they can watch. The leader introduces the equipment (often a board and some men in beginning position) and briefly states the objective of the game. "I try to get all of my men from this side to that side before anyone else does the same," or "I try to capture his men and keep him from capturing mine," or "I try to surround him and he tries to move past me."

Then the leader generally makes the first move. In subsequent moves, the leader must keep two things in mind: 1) The demonstration should be short; 2) It is the leader's responsibility to set up moves for the advantage of the opponent so that he can demonstrate situations, strategy, alternatives.

The leader can not anticipate that certain playing situations will arise automatically, nor should he talk about situations which do not arise; that will only confuse the learners. Thus he sets up situations through his own plays. Any person mature enough to understand the strategy of a table game will understand that the leader is setting up situations where he will be "caught." Therefore, the leader admits he is doing this by saying, "Now look what can happen if I move over here," or "Here is an example showing how my opponent can force me into a position which is advantageous for him." The onlookers will appreciate that the demonstration is a demonstration, not an exhibition of the leader's playing ability.

Many leaders, used to competing to win, find it very difficult to make moves which are strategically devastating. They keep seeing moves they can make to outplay their neophyte opponent. It may take a little practice to become the teacher rather than the player. The leader must remember constantly that his job is to direct attention to others, not to solicit their attention to his own prowess.

The leader is usually the loser and sometimes a second game may be played for demonstration without explanation. Here again, the leader, in order to expedite matters and in order to test the opponents' acuity sets up moves to his own disadvantage. In most cases, the onlookers will associate with the learners and oppose the leader. This is not because the leader is unpopular. It is an indication that the learners are vicariously the volunteer opponents and are pitting their wits against the leader to see how well they too have learned. The spectators then become kibitzers who help the players (unless they request otherwise). After the demonstrations, game equipment may be issued to those spectators who wish to play and the leader can move from group to group to help with further rules interpretation.

"Success is not in never failing; it is in rising each time you fall."
—Chinese Proverb

Chapter 4
Classification of Recreational Activities

Every planner of recreational events needs to be able to select activities which will ensure a well-rounded program. Activities which are too similar will offer the participants no change of pace, no variety, no chance to learn new skills, no chance to try out new and different actions and, in fact, will cheat the participant out of much of the joy he is entitled to through recreational programs. Further, a leader who offers only one type of activity assumes that all the participants enjoy activities of that type. The truth is, some participants may drop out of a program early if they see no chance to participate in an activity more of their choosing.

The purpose, then, of classifying recreational activities as presented here is to enable the leader to learn how to analyze the activities in order that he may avoid offering a program made up of all similar events.

There are several recognized methods of classifying recreational activities which are not recommended here for they tell us nothing about the component parts of the activities. Classification of activities by age tells us nothing about the activity except that it may be recommended for one age group. This in itself is a poor way to categorize recreational events for it denies the possibility of adapting the activity to another age and it assumes that all persons of a similar age are alike in ability, interest and knowledge. Classification by sex or grade level is similarly impractical for recreational purposes. The method of classifying activities presented here is based on that of Elmer Mitchell and Bernard Mason in "The Theory of Play" published in 1934. (It has since then been revised by Sapora and Mitchell in "The Theory of Play and Recreation," Ronald Press, New York.) Basically, their idea was that activities can be classified by form, movement, and interest or motivation. Because motivation is a moot question, and since recreation leaders are in no position to determine what factors motivate people, this portion of the classification is not recommended here.

Any recreational activity can be analyzed by movement and form by use of the following outline:

I. Classification According to Movement
  A. Motor Activity
    1. Fundamental (large muscle) Movement
      a. Locomotion
        (1) Moving in a horizontal plane (running, walking, dancing, crawling, skipping, etc.)
        (2) Moving in a vertical plane (climbing, jumping, etc.)
        (3) Moving through use of a vehicle (sledding, skating, swinging, bicycling, etc.)
      b. Handling Objects (throwing, catching, kicking, hitting, carrying, rolling, etc.)
    2. Accessory (small muscle) Movement
      a. Voice (singing, yodeling, cheering)
      b. Fingers (playing guitar, piano, knitting, whittling)
  B. Sensory Activity
    1. Sight
    2. Sound
    3. Touch
    4. Feel
    5. Taste
  C. Intellectual Activity

II. Classification According to Form
  A. Non-Competitive Activities
    1. Creative Activities
      a. With Materials
      b. Without Materials
    2. Roving Activities
    3. Hunting Activities
    4. Imitative Activities
    5. Social Activities
    6. Acquisitive Activities
    7. Aesthetic Activities
    8. Vicarious Activities
    9. Curiosity

  B. Competitive Activities
    1. Games
      a. Low organization
      b. Team games
      c. Combatants
      d. Dual games
      e. Mental games (table games)
    2. Contests
      a. Relays
      b. Individual
      c. Group

In order to use the outline a few explanations are necessary. Any recreational activity is primarily one of three forms of movement. It can not be denied that motor, sensory and intellectual movements are all involved in all recreational activities; however, it must be recognized that each activity utilizes one form of movement to a greater extent than the others.

CLASSIFICATION BY MOVEMENT

Motor activity involves use of muscles for the success of the activity. Fundamental muscles are the large muscles used to move the body or another object; accessory muscles are the small muscles which can manipulate or produce sounds, but which do not move large objects.

Fundamental muscle movement is divided into two parts: locomotion or moving the body itself from one place to another, and handling objects by propelling them or receiving them. There are many ways of locomotion. Some require additional body extensions in the form of skis, skates, bicycles, etc. Under locomotion come: running, jumping, dancing, skipping, dodging, climbing, swimming, canoeing, hopping, leaping, crawling, walking, gliding, and many others.

Handling objects through the use of large muscles entails hands and arms, back and legs and often auxiliary equipment such as bats, racquets, gloves, clubs, cues, etc. Included under handling objects would be: throwing, kicking, batting, rolling, catching, hitting.

If an activity involves muscles but does not involve large muscles, it would be classified as an accessory muscle movement. Playing the guitar, knitting, whittling, etc. involve the small manipulative muscles of the hand. Singing involves the voice and lungs.

If any activity is not primarily based on motor action it would be classified as either a Sensory Activity or an Intellectual Activity. The Sensory Activities are those depending primarily on one or more of the five basic senses: sight, sound, touch, smell and taste. The intellectual Activities are those which place the major emphasis upon the thought process.

Using the above system we can classify the movement of all recreational activities. Examples are:

Bowling: Movement: Motor activity, Fundamental movement, handling objects, rolling.

Tag: Movement: Motor activity, Fundamental movement, locomotion, running, and dodging.

Rollerskating: Movement: Motor activity, Fundamental movement, locomotion, use of auxiliary equipment.

Knitting: Movement: Motor activity, Accessory movement, fingers.

Listening to the Symphony: Movement: Sensory activity, Listening.

Analyzing the Symphony: Movement: Intellectual.

Checkers: Movement: Intellectual.

With activities such as enjoying music, art or literature it may be debatable whether appreciation is attained through the senses or the intellect but it is generally agree that keen senses are of primary importance and the intellect can not be used if the senses do not impart the proper messages. Therefore classification of appreciation is by senses. Analysis of music, however, is an intellectual activity.

The senses of touch, taste, and smell are used in social games where participants try to guess what objects are through the sense of touch or taste or smell only. For example, opaque vials of common seasonings and spices may be passed among a group, each member of which is to identify the contents of the vials by odor alone. It is amazing how many people fail to recognize cinnamon, cloves, nutmeg, anise, vinegar, etc. (One word of caution: garlic or onion should be passed around last or not at all for they will mask other odors.)

All a person need do in classifying according to movement is to decide whether the action emphasizes muscles, senses or the mental process and then define the movement as much as possible.

CLASSIFICATION BY FORM

Classification by form follows the same process as classification by movement. First the classifier needs to determine whether the activity is competitive or non-competitive. Competitive events entail an opponent or opponents engaged in the same activity.

In some activities such as mountain climbing there may be a competitor present in the form of one's self and whether this is competitive or not may be a matter of attitude or purpose.

If the activity is non-competitive, it will take one of nine forms. (1) Creative play involves the creative process using either materials such as craft work, sculpture, sewing, woodworking for the final product, or using no materials other than the paper on which the creative effort is recorded. Any kind of literary or musical composition is creative without materials.

Non-Competitive Forms

(2) Roving activities are those which include bicycling, exploring, hiking, touring, and sightseeing. (3) Hunting activities refer to funting, fishing, rock hunting, and the like. (4) Imitative activities are the dramatic events from children's finger plays to simple imitations to charades to dramatic roles.

(5) Social activities are those which may include many types of recreation but in which people are motivated to participate because of a desire to socialize. Parties, picnics, and banquets are social. (See Chapter 8). (6) Acquisitive activities include collections, while (7) aesthetic activities are those enjoyed for their form or beauty. (8) Vicarious activities are those in which the participant experiences events through imagining himself

in the role of another. Watching a Wild West movie and identifying with the hero is vicarious experience. Listening to a ghost story and becoming frightened is a vicarious experience as is weeping through the emotional scenes of a movie or play.

(9) Under curiosity, are classified activities such as solving a puzzle, reading, experimenting.

Competitive Forms

Competitive activities are divided into two categories: games and contests. It is important that the recreation planner understand the differences between these two for they are definite and each is needed for a well-rounded program.

Contests

Contests are characterized by offering the contestant no strategy which outwits his opponent, no choice and no interference with his opponent. Archery, golf and bowling are good examples of true contests, for in none of these does the contestant do anything which interferes with the opponent. There may be strategy in how to pick up a split in bowling, what club to use in golf, or how to allow for the wind in archery. This type of strategy and choice is individual and has nothing to do with interfering with the success of the other players. There is no deception in a contest.

A well-conducted relay is a true contest for each player is given a specific set of directions to follow. If the directions are not precise, and some players discover ways to do the action faster, the relay becomes a game of strategy. A true relay involves no strategy; the players have no choice as to how to do the activity and one player should never interfere with another. This is why relay teams should each have their own playing areas and goals, and be far enough apart so that no player interferes with another player.

Other true contests include: simple foot races, most track events, swimming races, jack stones, jump rope contests, competitive art, competitive music, self-testing events, and any activity where there is no interference with the opponent, no deception and no strategy.

Games

A game, on the other hand, is characterized by the factors of choice, strategy and interference with the progress of the opponent. A game is full of unexpected situations, strategy and deception. In a game the objective is to prevent the opponent from scoring or reaching a goal. In a contest the objective is to reach the goal sooner or with a better score than the opponent but without interfering with him.

Games may be of several types.

Low organized games are those with few rules, simple skills and very little cooperation among players on each team. Examples are: Tag, Hide and Seek, Midnight, Crows and Cranes.

Team games involve many rules, highly developed skill and great cooperation among members of each team.

Examples are: Baseball, Volleyball, Basketball, and Football.

Table games may be low organized games and may involve accessory muscle movement (i.e. Pick Up Sticks) but they are usually mental activities. Table games are usually mental strategy games played on special boards or charts. Checkers, Monopoly, Bridge, are some table games.

A combatant activity is an event between two persons which involves strategy and interference. Although they are often referred to as contests, Boxing, Fencing, and Wrestling are true combatant games.

Dual-Individual games are those in which two people or two pairs of people oppose each other. Tennis and Badminton are the activities usually thought of as dual-individual games.

A lead-up game may be a modification of a team game which resembles a game of low organization. Or it may be an improvised simple team game. Specifically, a lead-up game is one which serves to develop the basic skills used in a more complicated game. Keep Away on the most elementary level, is a lead-up game for basketball IF the leader is using the game to develop the competitive spirit found between two teams competing for possession of the ball. There are many games which serve as skill developing lead-ups for Basketball, Baseball, Soccer, etc.

EXAMPLES OF CLASSIFICATION

Completion of the classification of the activities listed on page 35 follows.

Bowling Movement: Motor activity, fundamental movement, handling objects, rolling
Form: Competitive, contest

Tag Movement: Motor activity, fundamental movement, locomotion, running and dodging
Form: Competitive, game, low organization

Roller-skating Movement: Motor activity, fundamental movement, locomotion, use of auxiliary equipment
Form: Non-competitive, roving (or, in the case of figure-skating, probably imitative)

Knitting Movement: Motor activity, accessory movement, fingers
Form: Non-competitive, creative, with material

Symphony Listening Movement: Sensory activity, listening
Form: Non-competitive, aesthetic

Symphony Analysis Movement: Intellectual
Form: Non-competitive, curiosity

Checkers Movement: Intellectual
Form: Competitive, game, table

By knowing many activities and how to classify them, the leader can readily see that a program consisting of Hide and Seek, Crows and Cranes, Midnight, and Steal the Bacon lacks variety, for all are low-organized games of fundamental movement involving running, tagging and dodging.

A better selection of activities would be: Rattlesnake Tag, In the Pond, Crows and Cranes and a few relays.

Because of the interference and deception involved, some people prefer games to contests and vice versa. Because of their nature and interests, some people prefer non-competitive to competitive activities. And because of individual differences, all people do not feel the same toward physical, mental or sensory activities. Even if all people as a group did prefer games involving large muscle activity, a recreational program without variety would soon be satiating.

The more a leader understands the component parts of a series of recreational activities, the better program planner he can be.

"Things excellent are as difficult as they are rare."
—Anon.

Chapter 5
Relays

To the general public, a well-led series of relays appears to be such a simple operation that the conclusion is that anyone could step in and conduct equally successful relays. On the other hand, a poorly run series of relays, leads spectators to comment on the obvious lack of control that the leader exerts over the participants. Upon analysis it is found that, of all informal competitive recreational activities, relays require the most precise instructions and leading methodology.

A true recreational relay is a contest among several teams, each individual member of which executes a pre-designated action in turn. The winner of the relay is the team whose members first complete their assigned functions. In-as-much as a true relay is a contest, the leader must make sure, through precise directions, that all strategy, choice, and interference are impossible. If the leader has given adequate instructions, no contestant should be able to think of a way to complete his turn faster through use of strategy. Any relay which involves choice, strategy or interference becomes a game and is thus removed from true relay status.

Any relay may involve locomotion or object handling or a combination of each. A relay based on locomotion requires each contestant to move from one location to another in a prescribed manner, i.e. run, crawl, slide, hip, etc. A non-locomotion or object handling relay requires that each contestant manipulate an object so that it goes from him to another contestant on his team. The object may be handed, rolled, kicked, thrown, etc. If the relay requires the contestant to move from his location after releasing the object, this is still considered a non-locomotion relay as the success of the team does not depend on the speed or manner in which the contestant moves after releasing the object. Some relays require locomotion while handling the object, i.e. carrying a bean balanced on a knife, bouncing a ball throughout a pre-designated course.

Because of the many possible movements or combinations of movements, relays are adaptable to and suitable for a wide variety of situations. Because they involve team interest, they are not well suited for most youngsters below the age of nine; however, they can be used in various forms for all ages above that.

RELAY FORMATIONS

There are five basic relay formations, each of which has merit in specific situations.

Simple File

The most common relay formation is the simple file which consists of several teams forming parallel lines with the first contestants in each team situated in, or behind, designated starting lines. (See Figure 1) In a file relay involving locomotion, turning areas are located in front of and equidistant from each team. There are times when it is advantageous to establish end lines for the last man in line to stand on or behind, and occasionally a spot may be designated for each individual player to stand on.

The action of the file relay with locomotion consists of each team member in turn moving to and around the turning spot, and returning to his team whereupon, after the proper hand-off signal, the next player takes his turn. In a non-locomotion relay, an object is passed from the first player to the next in a designated manner and so on until the object reaches the last man. (It is possible to start the object at either end of the file.) In some cases the relay ends when the last man receives the object. In other cases the object is returned to the first man by handing it back down the line in a designated manner and then the relay ends. In a third possibility, the last man carries the object to the front of the line and starts it down the line again. In this case, the relay is over when the object has traversed the line of players a pre-designated number of times. Each of these relay actions may be used, with slight modification, in each of the other four relay formations.

Advantages of the file relay include ease in organizing and controlling, facility in judging winners, and the fact that, because it is well known, it is readily accepted by participants who find initial security in familiar activities. However, this familiar type of relay will be a disadvantage to a leader if he uses this to the exclusion of other types of relays. For practical purposes, this relay is best with no more than eight teams of eight each.

Shuttle

A variation of the file is the shuttle relay. Not to be confused with the track meet shuttle relay, the recreational shuttle relay consists of a number of parallel teams each of which is divided into two halves each facing the other across an area over which the action is to be performed. (See Figure 2).

In cases where the team halves are uneven, the relay should always be arranged so that the larger number of participants are all on the same side of the action; and action starts with the first man in the longer line.

The action of a shuttle relay involving locomotion calls for the first participant from the designated side of each half team to move across the action area as directed until he reaches the other half of his team. At this time he makes the hand-off signal and the first man in that line takes his turn.

In the shuttle relay without locomotion, an object is propelled from the first man in one line to the first man in the other. As soon as a player completes propelling the object, he steps to the rear of his line. Thus the receiving player can propel the object across the playing area to a new receiver.

The advantages of the shuttle type relay are the same as those for the file relay plus the fact that this relay can be used efficiently for as many as eight teams of twelve each. Often this relay form is used with large groups when it is more practical than the simple file relay.

Square

An unusual yet very useful variation of the simple file relay is the square relay (which may become a triangle, pentagon or hexagon if necessary.)

The participants in a square relay either stand or sit in four even files arranged with each of the four teams forming one side of a square and facing inward. The action of a square relay is the same as for the simple file relay and any of the variations for action with locomotion or non-locomotion is feasible.

In locating turning points for square relays with locomotion, it is better to have a separate point for each team rather than to have one turning point located in the center of the square. It is also necessary to mark the position of each end of the team so that the sides of the square will remain of equal length. (See Figure 3)

The square relay lends itself particularly well to situations where activity must be confined to a small space and to social situations. It is not a practical relay for strenuous activity nor can it accommodate groups larger than 32 without being extremely cumbersome and involving short turns with long waits. Ideally, the square relay is best suited for groups of 16 to 24. Another disadvantage of the square relay is that the leader must stand at one of the corners of the square, a position from which it is not possible to see all participants equally.

Spoke

While not used often, the spoke relay is not to be overlooked. Actually, this relay form is a variation of the simple file form with each team being arranged as one of several spokes in a wheel. There may be from four to eight spokes with from four to twelve participants per spoke. Ideally six to eight spokes with six to eight contestants is ample. In either locomotion or non-locomotion action, it is imperative to mark lines between which the team members must be located. (See Figure 4)

The action of the spoke relay may be the same as the simple locomotion or any of the three possible non-locomotion forms of the simple file relay.

The spoke relay has both advantages and disadvantages. It is not very practical for several reasons. It is very difficult for a leader to position himself so that he may be seen and heard equally by all during instruction. It is also difficult for the leader to watch the action and determine winners.

Locomotion type relays are also difficult for the contestants as centrifugal force is created when one runs around a circle. Unless the circle is large, runners tend to slip as they lean inward to counteract the force. It is also impossible to pass a contestant without moving around him, thus actually lengthening the course for the fast runner. Such violates the definition of a true relay, although in this case this is probably a minor point.

The advantage of the spoke relay lies in the fact that it is possible to use the spoke relay for very large groups competing in an athletic field, (i.e. over 100 participants). Several "wheels" composed of eight spokes each may be established and one leader may direct the activities from an elevation in the grand stand through use of a public address system. The winning teams in each "wheel" may form a winner's "wheel" for a final play off if such recognition is desired. With assistance, one may direct two or three hundred contestants through use of the spoke relays.

Circle

The circle relay form is unlike any of the preceding in that each team is arranged in an individual symmetrical circle around which all action for that team occurs. The players may each move in turn around the outside circumference of their own circle, or they may weave in and out around their own team members.

An object may be passed one or more times around the circle or it may go around the circle once in one direction and return to the starter in the opposite direction. A common non-locomotion circle relay action is a ball handling drill where each player in turn stands in the center of the circle and passes a ball to each team member, going around the entire circle once during his turn. (See Figure 5)

The greatest disadvantage to the circle relay is that each team must have a carefully marked circle on which to stand or the circle size will change, thus allowing strategy to enter the contest. Since the definition of a relay does not involve ability to win through strategy, such action should not be condoned. It must also be realized that it is hard for the leader to be seen by all the players during instruction. The main advantage of the circle relay appears to be its use for throwing, kicking, rolling, volleying, and other ball handling events. One advantage of a circle relay not found in any other form is that the formation of the players permits every contestant to see the members of his own team, not only all at once, but also face to face.

RELAY EXAMPLES

FIGURE 1. Simple File Relay with Six Teams of Six Each.

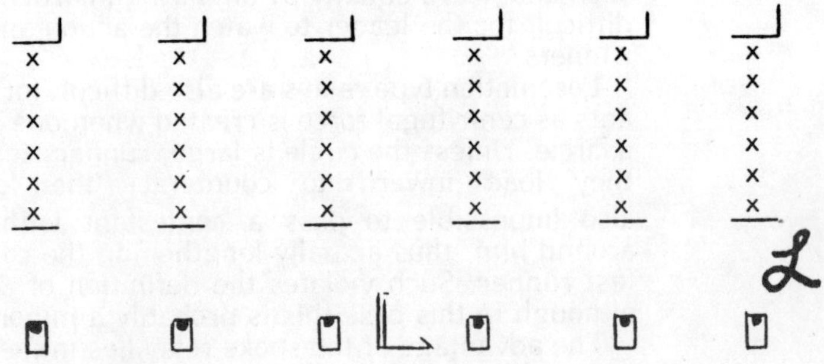

___ Starting Line

⌐ Optional Line for file non-locomotion

▯ Turning Point for file with locomotion

L Leader during explanation

𝓛 Leader during relay

FIGURE 2. Shuttle Relay with Four Teams of Nine Each.

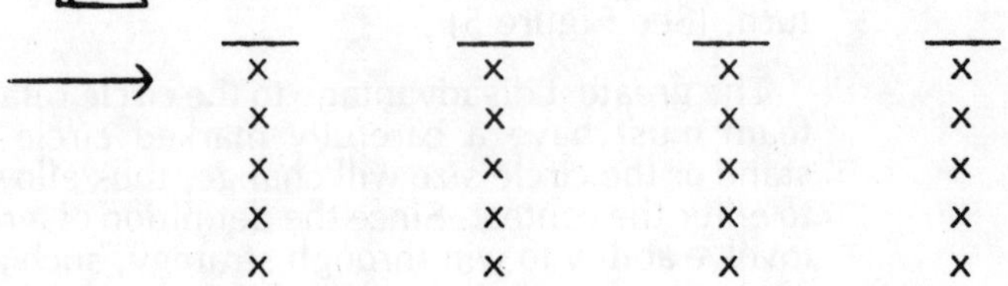

⟶ = Starting side (when teams can not have equal number on each side)

L = Position of leader

FIGURE 3. Square Relay with Four Teams of Six Each.

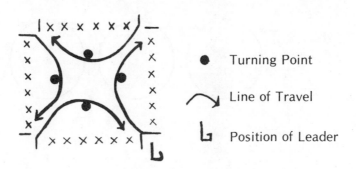

• Turning Point

Line of Travel

⌐ Position of Leader

FIGURE 4. Spoke Relay with Eight Teams of Six Each.

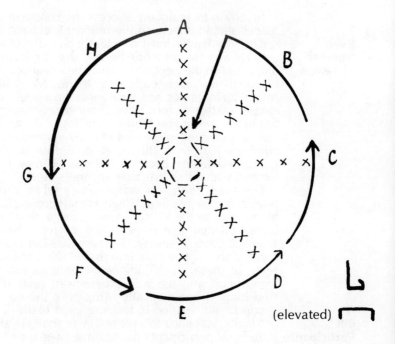

___ = Team Boundary Lines

↑ = Line of Travel of players from Team A (in locomotion-type relay)

⌐ = Position of Leader

FIGURE 5. Circle Relay with Four Teams of Ten Each.

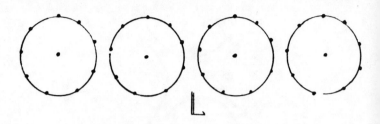

$\llcorner$ = Leader

GENERAL RULES FOR ORGANIZING RELAYS

In order to maintain success in conducting relays a leader should adhere to the following general aids:

Even Number of Teams

The play leader must constantly plan ahead for his next activity and the methods he will use for transition from one event to the next. Whenever it is practical, he should establish four, six or eight relay teams. Many times relays follow team games and vice versa. In either case, it is a simple matter to form four relay teams from two game teams, or two game teams from four, six or eight relay teams. Grouping into or out of uneven numbered teams is cumbersome. In addition, it is easier to direct even numbered teams because the leader may be centrally located without obstructing anyone's view.

However, there are some times when three or five teams may be justified. When a small group plays, uneven teams may be the logical answer. Certainly 12 players are better divided into three teams of four than into four teams of three. Likewise 15 players are better divided into three teams of five than into three teams of four plus one team of three. Such judgments become automatic with experience, and the well-experienced relay director will find himself automatically estimating the number in the group in anticipation of forming even teams.

6-8 Participants Per Team

Ideally, it is good to have no fewer than six and no more than eight participants per team. Fewer than six makes a very short relay (unless each takes two turns.) Having fewer than six players per team is not, however, an excuse for eliminating relay activities. More than eight participants tends to create a dull relay, for one may have 30 seconds of activity and four or five minutes of observation; and interest lags in even the most exciting of relays. If there are more than eight per team, the shuttle relay is probably best, with the circle form used for some activities.

At Least 3 Relays

Grouping teams for only one relay is a waste of time and automatically permits only one group to win. Having several relays allows losing teams new opportunities to excel and makes the activities of greater interest. The maximum number of relays to hold at any one time depends on the circumstances. Age, interest, occasion and time all enter the decision. Probably, if the relays are a part of a fairly lengthy program, 30 minutes is a hearty maximum. This, however, is only a generality. The author has seen a clever leader direct relays for one hour and stop amid requests for more, but such is the exception.

Keep Same Formation While leaders need to be familiar with all five relay formations and should vary their programs by using all of them, the changes should not be at the expense of participant time. Going from one formation to another just for the sake of variety is time-consuming beyond justification, unless at least four relays have been conducted in the previous formation and four more are to be conducted in the new formation.

SPECIFIC STEPS FOR LEADING RELAYS

The secret to successful relays is precise directions. Many times, losers' accusations that the winners "cheated" are brought about by inadequate directions which either made the action unclear or which invited initiative and strategy. One of the values is that anyone can participate without having to think!

The following ten steps are guides for successful relays.

Establish Boundaries Prior to giving any directions, the leader must establish the lines between which he wishes the contestants to stand, and turning points for locomotion relays. It is a certain indication of lack of preparation if the leader is not precise in positioning the teams.

When considering the relay, the leader must also plan his equipment and be sure it is ready and close at hand before the relay teams are positioned. Keeping teams ready while sorting out, seeking or organizing equipment is a sure way to lose interest, attention and control. Relay equipment should consist of exactly identical items for each team. If breakable items are used (such as inflated balloons which must remain intact) extras on hand will prevent what might otherwise be a discouraged team.

Form Teams In forming relay teams it is efficient to have the first person in each line count the number of people in his group, including himself, and report to the leader. Then the leader may look to make sure that the boys and girls (or men and women) are equally distributed and that no one team has an unfair advantage due to size, age, agility, etc.

If teams are uneven, one person on the smaller teams should have two turns. Each new relay should find a different person having the second turn, not as much to prevent fatigue as to give equal chance to others. If one team has one extra player, he may be used as a judge, as a starter, or as an equipment clerk; however, he should serve for only one turn. A different person from the same team should serve as assistant on successive relays.

Give Directions

When giving relay directions what to do is not sufficient; how to do it must be added. For example, if the directions are, "Carry a dried bean on a knife," many different ways of carrying it can occur including moving it close to the handle, putting the thumb on it, using one hand under the blade to steady it, etc. Better directions would mention one hand behind the back except when picking up a dropped bean, no holding the bean on, bean placed on the top of the knife, etc.

The leader needs to think through his directions in advance and think of every way possible that his own words would be interpreted. The leader needs to put himself in the position of an eager participant ready to do anything permitted to help his team.

In giving the directions, the leader must be brief or interest will lag. He must give his exact directions in a manner which is pleasing, appealing, and perhaps humorous. There are individual ways of explaining why "You can't touch the bean with your thumb," which arouse antagonism and there are ways which elicit a desire to cooperate.

The director, always aware of safety, can help control accidents through careful selection of the relay and through careful directions. Attention should be given to explaining the direction of travel. In file and shuttle relays involving locomotion, runners may be told to go to the right of the turning point or the other half of his team, thus reducing some chaos. (Note: many excited participants will forget, but no penalty should be imposed.) In circle and spoke relays involving locomotion, the contestants must be told whether action is clock-wise or counter-clock-wise and shown visually which way to run, as "clock-wise," "counter-clock-wise," "right," and "left," are always misinterpreted by someone.

Error Procedure

In a recreational relay, if an error occurs, if equipment is dropped, if a step is missed, the player will have lost enough time in making this mistake. He should never be penalized by being made to start over again. He should start from the exact spot where the error occurs. Players will never then be criticized by team-mates for continual errors of "dropping the ball" just before finishing a turn and being required to start over again.

Relays which require those making errors to return to the starting place and begin anew should be reserved for athletic skill drills where mistakes can not be tolerated and players must be precise. Recreational relays are neither drills nor training devices and the consequences of errors are to be minimized.

Explain Transfer Signal

Many times, in their eagerness to take their turns, children will start running before their predecessor returns. Or sometimes a runner, in his eagerness to be fair, will delay in starting, much to the consternation of his teammates. Several methods are used for sending the next runner on his way. A common one is for the returning runner to tag the outstretched hand of the next participant as he returns. Sometimes, however, the next participant steps forward to meet his returning teammate, an action which a neighboring team finds "unfair." More often, though, the returning runner misses the outstretched hand and has to go back for it. Handing an object to the next runner is a good way to transfer the action.

When the teams are even, a good signal transfer method is for the returning runner to go to the end of the line and either pass an object, i.e. baton, ball, etc., to the person in front of him or tap that person on the shoulder. The object or tap is thus passed up the line until it reaches the first runner who is waiting, ready for his turn. An advantage of this method is that it keeps each team member alert and playing an active role even when not taking his turn.

Demonstrate If feasible the leader can demonstrate the relay action, including direction of travel and transfer of action signal. Or the relay may be practiced by the first man in each team. This way the leader can look for errors and correct them. One entire team should never be used for demonstration purposes because it gives them the unfair advantage of a practice run. In complicated relays, it may be well to let all teams have a practice run just as if it were a real race, then play it again "for real."

Start/End Signals Contestants need to know when to start and how to let the leader know they have finished. It is not fair warning for the leader to say suddenly, "1-2-3-Go!" unless the players know that will be the starting signal. Participants should be informed that the starting signal will be: "Ready, get set, go" or "One-two-three-go" or "One-two-three" Blow (use of whistle).

Just the single word "Go!" gives no warning and some are always caught asleep! One needs to watch "false starts" and should start the relay anew after recalling runners who "jump the gun."

The ending signal is the method used by the teams to signal the leader or judges that their turns are completed. So that the judges are sure to see this immediately, the team should execute some action so different from what they were doing previously that it is impossible to miss it. This is generally called an "explosive" action and is executed by the entire team simultaneously. Several actions are possible:

a) When the last man is finished, everyone on the team sits down on the floor, or ground, simultaneously with hands folded.
b) Teams seated in chairs may all raise arms simultaneously. (All rising simultaneously usually results in tipped-over chairs!)
c) The entire team turns an about face and stands with arms on the shoulder of the man in front.

d) The last man to run carries a red flag which he waves at the end of his turn.

Questions   If directions were complete but brief there should not be any.

Start Relay   Using the signal explained in Step 7, start the relay. If it is a shuttle relay with teams divided unevenly, (e.g. five on one side and four on the other) start the relay with the first man on the larger side, so each will get one turn and end up in the same order.

Recognize Winners   First and second place winners should always be recognized. Third place may be recognized if they wish and if more than four teams compete. It is a matter of individual judgment what to do if all teams are finished except one or perhaps two who are struggling onward. It is always advisable not to go on to the bitter end, as many participants find it embarrassing to be subjected to the observation of the rest of the group as they struggle to complete their turns. Others, on the other hand, feel particularly hurt if "robbed" of their turns and insist on being allowed time to complete the relay. Consequently, if it appears to the leader that the last teams or two do not wish to have their turns completed, then the slogan, "Don't go on to the bitter end," is best heeded. Otherwise, let those who wish to finish have their fun.

Summary of Steps   It would seem that relay leading is a complicated matter; yet, if the ten simple steps are understood, the process is simple. Briefly then, the steps for leading relays are: 1) Establish boundaries; 2) Form teams; 3) Give directions; 4) Explain procedure for errors; 5) Explain the transfer signal; 6) Demonstrate; 7) Explain starting and ending signals; 8) Ask for questions; 9) Start the relay; 10) Recognize the winners.

CHOOSING THE RELAY

As in all recreational activities chosen by the leader, care must be taken to select relays that are wholesome, healthy, safe and in the best interest of all participants. In spite of the fact that some relays look good on paper, they are not recommended for actual use because of health or safety factors.

A popular relay, generally called "Driving the Pig to Market" consists of propelling a soft drink bottle across the relay area with a small wand or stick. The action itself is quite harmless, yet the bottles roll in a crooked line and bottles from opposing teams often collide. When this happens, the bottles can break with a force which sprays minute strands of glass over a large area generally occupied by players. This same activity can be conducted using empty soft drink cans, or wooden dowels instead of breakable glass, thus eliminating a dangerous hazard.

Other questionable relays involve passing an orange held under the chin from person to person without use of the hands, or passing a lifesaver from person to person each of whom stands with his hands behind his back and a toothpick held between his teeth, or passing a match box from person to person—or rather from nose to nose—using no hands. In each case the health element must be considered, since respiratory diseases can be spread from person to person through such close personal contact.

While these relays are intended to break down social reserve and make people feel better acquainted, relays involving such close personal contact often serve the opposite purpose and make people feel uncomfortable, embarrassed and alienate them toward further participation in relay activities. A leader who has empathy with the feelings of individuals can imagine the discomfort caused by body odor, bad breath, poor complexion, small chins, large noses, and shyness when relays involving such close contact are directed.

Any time a recreation activity becomes an embarrassment, it ceases to become recreation and actually does the participants an unforgivable disservice. There are literally hundreds of wholesome, enjoyable relays than can be conducted successfully. They are among the most popular and frequent of informal recreational activities. It is up to the leader to choose and lead them well.

"Walk carefully;
someone may be
following in your
footsteps."
—Anon.

Chapter 6
Music and Rhythm

It can not be denied, Music is the universal language. People everywhere hum, whistle, sing, tap their feet, drum their fingers. Without rhythm, our lives would be incomplete. Music belongs in a recreation program: the playground, the summer camp, the senior citizens center, the community center, the party, the picnic. There is no reason why we can not have music, for music depends not upon what is with us, but what is within us.

The equipment for music may be carried with us. Voices make it possible to carry on a musical program with no additional equipment, although instruments and phonographs enhance the program and increase its scope. No special space is needed; music can take place indoors or outdoors on any surface, or any shaped area. No experience is needed; even beginners can find success in musical activities. Anyone and everyone can participate for music knows no age, size, shape, or sex limitation. The musical program can be varied to fit any situation, any time, any place, any event for anyone.

WHY MUSIC?

It is logical to analyze music to see what qualities it contains to make it so universally appealing. First of all, for reasons unknown, music is enjoyable. But beyond that, music has certain unique qualities. It is the great unifier for, through music, people become one. All reflect the mood of the song—serious, happy, humorous, appreciative, patriotic. Whatever it is, music unifies our thoughts, our actions and our moods.

Music is an equalizer, too. In music all are alike. There are no boundaries of wealth or race or creed. Nor are there newcomers, strangers, young or old. All feel a kinship through a song.

Music allows opportunity for self-expression. One can whistle, hum or sing his happiness; music can be a positive catharsis for any emotion. Beyond these reasons, music has beauty; it is pleasing to the ears; it seems to help satisfy our need for the aesthetic.

The scope of music is wide and it can be integrated with many other programs. Music is to be acted, through action songs, action ballads or operetta. Action songs are those in which motions are used to indicate the words. They are always simple and they are great favorites with boys and girls. Music is for games and contests. Many games are singing games; some activities require rhythm but no words. Through music we can imagine, remember, believe and appreciate. Music is more than these. Music is for listening, for playing, for creating. It is for everyone, for all times, for all places.

TO LEAD A SONG

A song leader is not the same as a song teacher. The song leader may assume that the majority of his participants know the song and his job is to lead it. A song teacher, on the other hand, may assume that few if any know the song and his responsibility is to teach it so all know it.

The beginning song leader needs two things before he starts his first song leadership. A belief in music and its value is the first prerequisite for a song leader; for his enthusiasm will show through his leadership. If he believes in the activity and shows it, his possible ineptness may not show in his enthusiasm.

A second attribute of a song leader is a repertoire of songs he is prepared to lead without notes, words or reference to a book, card or sheet of paper. When the leader uses props in song leading, he loses his contact with his audience, and consequently ceases to lead them. He may have a repertory (storehouse) of songs to which he can refer between leadership times; however, on the job he needs his ready supply of songs.

Leading the song itself is really one of the easiest of all leadership skills. If one can talk, one can sing. If one can lead a game, one can lead a song. Someone once remarked facetiously, "There are three rules for leading a song. One, start when they start. Two, end when they end. And, three, sing the same song they sing." Actually this is not far from the truth as one can see watching a 12-year-old lead "America" at a camp flag raising ceremony.

The major objective in leading a song is really to start the group together, to keep them together and to end the song all together. In leading a song, one assumes that the group already knows the song and merely need to be reminded what note to start on and how fast to sing. If the leader is not sure of the note, he can hum a few bars to himself and try it out before giving the audience the note. Or he can summon help from one of the singers who will gladly volunteer a note.

The matter of starting the group is simple, but keeping them together seems to be the biggest problem for the neophyte. He never seems to know what to do with his hands. Many books tell what to do for 3/4 time or 2/4 or 4/4 or even 6/8 time, but this seems to frighten the beginner. He probably doesn't know what the time signatures mean and usually has no one to ask. He possibly is too unskilled to determine the song's time by listening. There are, however, three different types of hand motion for the unsophisticated song leader which are simple, require no knowledge of music, and which are successful.

Beat Leading

Some songs lend themselves naturally to a leading technique called, for the lack of anything more descriptive, the Beat Technique. Here the leader uses his hand (or hands) to beat the normal cadence of the song. He may beat from side to side or up and down. If he has trouble determining if the song has a ready "beat" or not, he should practice by tapping his foot or drumming his fingers. If he can do this evenly, he can beat time with his hand. It can be seen that some songs are readily led by the beat method. For example, the following songs are naturally accented and can be led by the beat method on the words designated.

The More We Get Together, Row, Row, Row Your Boat, Three Blind Mice

Level Leading

After beating the music, most leaders find themselves moving automatically into level leading which is simply using the position of the hand to indicate whether the note is higher or lower than it was before. Actually, the leader indicates each syllable as it is sung by changing the level of his hand in the direction of the tune. As the tune goes up, so does the hand; as the pitch descends, so does the hand. This type of leading is unconsciously automatic with most people. Of course, one can not level lead if the group is singing rounds or harmony. Beat leading will work there successfully.

Using level leading as a guessing game can prove its effectiveness. A leader can think through a song to himself and "lead" it by using his hand to rise and fall with his thoughts. The group can then guess what he is leading, particularly if he gives them a few hints. If he says, Patriotic song and level leads "America" as he thinks it, over 50 percent of the group should guess it correctly. For a round, try "Row, Row, Row Your Boat"; for a Christmas song, try "Silent Night." These three are easily recognized especially if the hints are given. The leader can then try others.

Action Leading

A third method of song leading is one which is used with informal action songs. Action songs are those in which both singers and leaders do something with their hands to act out the words of the song. The leader who may feel uncomfortable beating time or leading by pitch level often finds action songs the answer to the problem of what to do with the hands. Some leaders do not like action songs because they usually require some histrionics which they do not enjoy. Others find the dramatic appeal of the action song a logical way to overcome the self-consciousness which accompanies their first attempts to lead.

Examples of action songs include:
My Hat It Has Three Corners
In a Cottage in a Woods
If You're Happy and You Know It
One Finger, One Thumb
Itsy Bitsy Spider
Lady and the Crocodile

Leading Control

A good song leader not only leads the singing, he controls the quality of the music. He knows that music is never synonymous with noise and that shouting is not singing. Contests wherein groups try to sing louder than other groups are not quality programs and should always be discouraged.

The choice of song is often up to the leader. He can be very discriminating and have a musical program of high quality. Some songs do not deserve the efforts of a leader. Many so called popular songs are hard to sing because of the unusual melodies and many are not suitable or acceptable for group singing. College drinking songs and ballads referring to drink, sex, drugs or crime are not suitable for boys and girls on playgrounds or in camps; nor are they acceptable to the middle or senior aged groups. Many songs which high school and college-age youth enjoy should not be selected by a paid leader. The youth may sing the songs in their own groups, but a leader is hired to maintain or improve quality and must be discriminating in his taste.

Another thing which leaders must control is the tempo of the song. Too often the unperceptive leader will permit the group to lead him making already slow songs into dirges, or jazzed-up fast songs beyond the semblance of music. The perceptive leader sets the tempo and permits no song to drag needlessly or race out of control.

The leader is also responsible for the pitch of the song. Some songs are often started on a note which seems logical, only to be completely out of the range of most singers on the high notes which follow. "The Star Spangled Banner" is a prime example of this. The lines, "Oh, say can you see . . . ," must be pitched low or the singers will never reach the notes of "And the rockets' red glare."

Another example—a popular camp song—is "Peace of the River." In this song, it seems logical to pitch the song relatively high; however, by the time the song is half over, it is obvious that no one can reach, "From the hills I gather courage" and instead of music, one is leading laughter, giggles or groans.

Until he can do it automatically, the song leader might make himself some cue notes of songs with high notes in the middle so he will remember to start low. In case he does start out on the wrong note, the leader should always stop the song and start again.

Often novice songleaders find that once they start a song high, they think high and can not re-start at a lower note. At times like this there is always someone in the group who will volunteer a note. Using such a volunteer only helps to emphasize the group work involved in singing.

TEACHING SONGS

In teaching songs it is important that the singers develop interest in the song and that they are successful in learning at least a part of it on the first lesson so that they will look forward to singing it again. The success or failure of a new song very often depends on the way it was presented to the group. A wise leader studies his material before he introduces it and, as in the introduction of games, he arouses interest by a unique introduction.

If he does not know much about the song or its origin he should never invent stories, though. For example introducing a song by saying, "We are now going to learn 'Kookaburra,' " violates all principles of introduction. It certainly is authoritarian and arouses no interest among persons to whom "Kookaburra" is a meaningless word. Likewise, "The next song is about a monkey eating gum-drops," is an equally poor introduction. It is not only not factual but shows that the leader disrespects group singing enough to affect knowledge he does not have. A more factual introduction would be: "There is an Australian bird which has a song like laughter. He perches in a eucalyptus tree which the Australians call a gum tree and he sounds as if he is the merriest bird in the forest (which the Australians call 'bush'). This is a song about this interesting bird."

Obviously, if the leader does not have access to such facts, the invention about the monkey and the gum drops is unforgiveable. In this situation, it is far better to intro-duce "Kookaburra" as a song which is fun to sing and which comes from Australia.

When teaching songs, it is imperative that the leader enunciate new or uncommon words. A child once asked a camp counselor, after singing "Peace of the River," "Who is Olivia?" The counselor, not having any idea, asked the child where she had heard the name. The youngster answered, "We've been singing 'Peace I Ask of Thee, Olivia.' " More than one child has sung, "Green Grow the Russians, Ho" instead of "Rushes." How many youngsters have just such strange ideas of the songs they sing is anyone's guess, but unless the adult working with them takes time to help them understand the meaning, or to define a specific word that is not yet in the child's vocabulary, these incidents are bound to be many. Many children sing, "Little Tommy Tinker sat on a clinker," without any idea whether a clinker is an insect, a custard pie or whatever the imagination can conjure up.

There are some children who are convinced (unfortunately) that they can not carry a tune. An excellent song which can dispel this fallacy is "Sarasponda." If the accompanying part which goes, "Boom dah, boom dah, boom dah" is taught first, everyone can participate with equal success. Then if the "Sarasponda" part is taught and the two sections sung together, the "non-singer" suddenly finds he can even harmonize!

When actually teaching the song, it is generally good to start by singing the entire song for the group. This helps them to think of the song as a whole and gives a good introduction. Then, sing a phrase (or two, if they are not too long) and have the group repeat it after you. In this way, the words and music are learned together, bit by bit. This method is known as "rote teaching" or "lining-out." The Puritans used this method of learning songs, since most of the singers did not possess books. There are modern records in existence, particularly of early American music, such as from the "Bay Psalm Book," using this "lining-out" method of teaching songs. In a song with several verses and a simple chorus, such as "Marching To Pretoria," it is well to teach the chorus first. In this way everyone singing the song is a successful participant immediately, even though he doesn't remember all the verses for a while.

If you feel ill at ease singing a song through alone, it is possible that some people already know the song and will help. All it takes is the request, "If you know the song, sing it through with me." If only a few know the song, and they are spread far apart, have them group together to lend strength and confidence to each other, as well as to you.

In teaching rounds, have the group sing the song through in unison two or three times, then divide into the number of groups needed. Be sure to announce in advance how many times each group is to sing the song through. A good rule of thumb is that it can be sung through as many times as you have groups. With rounds, as with other types of songs, though, stop the song while the interest is still high. The group will then be eager to sing it the next time.

Since children are imitators, the attitude you have toward the new song will be contagious. If you exhibit enthusiasm and it is obvious that you think the song is fun to sing and to learn, singers will quickly pick up this positive attitude. You may discover that each succeeding song you teach becomes easier. As the group begins eagerly to look forward to learning more new songs, your job as song leader/teacher becomes more satisfying by the day.

Use of song sheets for song leading and teaching should be limited. If the time does not allow for review or teaching, song sheets with printed words are justifiable.

In a camp, playground or youth group setting, however, song sheets detract from the program and from the leader. No one can possibly keep his eyes on a leader and a printed sheet simultaneously. Because of a fear of singing the wrong words, the singer will keep his eyes on the paper and the actions and efforts of the leader are wasted. Rustling papers, turning pages, and the tops of heads are all the leader sees.

As with any activity, leading and teaching songs requires some practice. No one ever becomes a song leader overnight and no song leader or teacher became proficient without making mistakes. In recreational singing, one can be forgiven mistakes in method. What is most important in recreational singing is the group unification through music of a positive type.

> *"If you have knowledge,*
> *let others light their*
> *candles at it."*
> —Margaret Fuller

Chapter 7
Tournaments

Tournaments are merely methods of organizing competitive activities. There are many types of tournaments because there are many reasons for competition, many types of competitive activities and many types of competitors. Not everyone desires to participate in organized competition, or in organized competition which culminates in the designation of a winner from a group of contestants. For those who do wish to participate in structured competition, the leader must be prepared to select the most desirable means of organizing the competition.

There are fundamentally three categories into which tournaments can be divided; although there are some miscellaneous types of tournaments which do not seem to fit any category. Each type of tournament is used for a specific purpose, and each type has its own advantages and disadvantages.

Tournaments can be used for most competitive activities for which several teams or players wish to determine a champion. Some activities, however, such as Four-Square Ball and Croquet, must have the rules changed for tournament use. Having four or more players competing against each other in one activity presents unique problems which dual or team activities do not have. Common tournament activities are: softball, bowling, volleyball, basketball, horseshoes, tennis, badminton, checkers, tetherball, marbles, table tennis, table games for two players or two teams.

SELF-PERPETUATING TOURNAMENTS

There are times when it is desirable to organize a tournament in which one can compete at different hours throughout the day, which has an undesignated number of games and which could, if permitted to, last an entire season or longer with little or no supervision. The self-perpetuating tournament or challenge tournament meets these specifications, and there are several kinds which are easily structured for informal competition. On the whole, challenge tournaments are less formal than other types, less structured and require little or no supervision. They are used for younger or less experienced contestants, for practice and to pick top players for more highly organized tournaments.

Ladder   The simplest self-perpetuating tournament is the ladder where players' names are arranged in a vertical column and any player may challenge either of the two players directly above himself. (See Figure 1.)

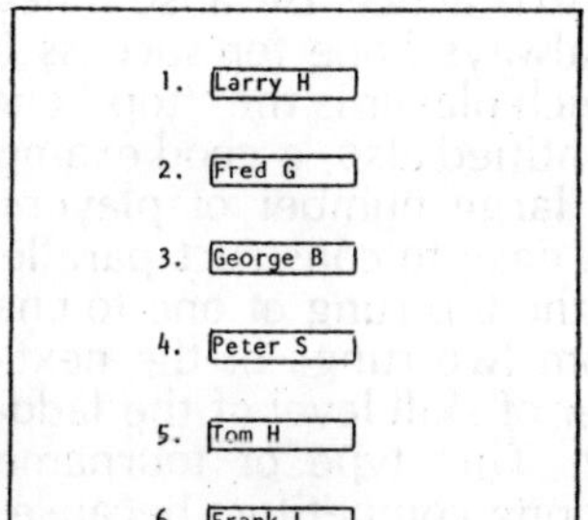

The player challenged must agree to play. In the event he refuses, his name is moved down to the challenger's position and the challenger moves up to his. Usually a challenged player accepts the challenge and the two play the number of games designated by the tournament rules, i.e. one, three, or five. The winner of the one game, or two out of three, or three out of five has his name moved to the higher position of the two names, or retains it in that position if it was there before the game. The object of the tournament is to move to the top "rung" of the ladder.

In order to designate in which order the names should be placed on the ladder before the first challenge, one of three methods may be used. The leader may arbitrarily place the names on the various rungs; participants' names may be drawn at random; or the participants may be scheduled in the order in which they sign up for the tournament. Placement at random is probably the most acceptable method.

1. Larry H
2. Fred G
3. George B
4. Peter S
5. Tom H
6. Frank L
7. Bill W
8. Don P
9. Don W
10. Andy A
11. Mike N
12. Joe S
13.
14.
15.

FIGURE 1.
Ladder Tournament

A tournament board may be constructed in several ways. A simple method is to use a piece of plywood with a pair of L hooks on which to hang each name tag. A name tag may be made by drilling a hole in each end of a tongue depressor and printing the name with a wood burning tool or a colored pencil or ball point pen. (Ink, felt tipped pens, or water paint will smear.) The name may also be painted on paper and taped to the tongue depressor.

Ladder Advantages Advantages of the ladder tournament lie in the fact that it is unsupervised. Once organized it can continue indefinitely. It is best to set a time limit, however, for interest will usually wane after about two weeks. This tournament helps to determine the better players who may then be selected as participants in a more highly structured tournament.

This tournament further maintains a continual chance for any competitor to practice. Because it never eliminates a player, there is always hope for success involved. It is also easy to see which player is the "top" one. Second and third are easily identified also, a good example of recognition. In case of a large number of players with a wide range of skill, it is easy to construct parallel ladders and permit players on the top rung of one to challenge one of those on the bottom two rungs of the next ladder to the right with the order of skill level of the ladders ascending from left to right. This type of tournament further is excellent for the young competitors because of the choice, hope, and self-involvement.

Ladder Disadvantages In spite of its advantages, the ladder tournament has some disadvantages. It is definitely limited to fewer than 25 players, preferably no more than 12 to 15. Poor players who remain constantly at the bottom are singled out and may be discouraged. Since this tournament is often used with beginning competitors, identification of the poorest player is not always conductive to a desire to compete any further.

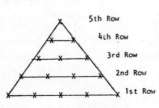

5th Row
4th Row
3rd Row
2nd Row
1st Row

The pyramid tournament is like the ladder tournament in that players on a lower level challenge those on the higher. This tournament, however, has the names arranged in pyramid form. The best minimum number of players is probably 15 or at least five rows to climb. (See Figure 2).

Pyramid **FIGURE 2. Pyramid Tournament**

In setting up the tournament, the number of rows used will be governed by the number of entries. Figure 2. Is set up for 15 contestants; however, the addition of one more row would accommodate 21 contestants, the addition of two rows would raise it to 28, and so on.

In operation, it employs the standard Ladder Tournament procedure; those on one row challenging those in the row above, and if successful in the challenge, taking the place of the contestant challenged in the row above. For example, a contestant in row two challenges a contestant in row three and defeats him, thus moving up to the spot in row three where the challenged contestant was. The defeated contestant from row three is then moved down to the spot on row two which was occupied by the challenger.

This tournament, like the standard Ladder Tournament, may be used as a basis for setting up teams by using the top three or six players to form a team. It is best used for individual competition, but may be used for competition.

Pyramid Advantages This tournament has the advantage over the ladder tournament of being able to accommodate more players efficiently on one chart. A pyramid of 28 is not too unwieldy; further, two pyramids of 14 each is a better tournament than two ladders of 14 each. At the lower levels the participant has a much greater choice of persons to challenge. Like the ladder tournament, the pyramid offers a continuous opportunity for practice. Unlike the ladder tournament, the pyramid does not single out one loser. All persons on the bottom row are equals. Psychologically, for younger players, there is a security and feeling of belonging engendered by being a member of a group of equals.

Pyramid Disadvantages Probably the greatest disadvantage of the pyramid tournament is the fact that its use in selecting top players for further competition or for awarding prizes is limited. Because there are two players on the second tier, there can be no designation of a second and a third place winner.

Several variations of the pyramid tournament are used either to accommodate larger groups or to initiate an element of elimination.

Funnel The most simple variation of the pyramid tournament is the funnel which consists of pyramid with a short ladder projecting from the apex.

King's Pyramid This tournament is for large groups. (See Figure 3.) The pyramid may be set up by placing participants at random on the pyramids or by placing the best players on the top pyramids.

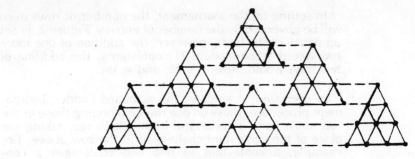

FIGURE 3. King's Pyramid
[for large groups]

In this tournament it is best if each pyramid be limited to ten players. Figure 3 shows six pyramids of ten contestants per pyramid, a total of 60 players. Each player may challenge someone directly above him in his own pyramid until he reaches the next to the top row. Here he may challenge either the top man on his own pyramid or one of the four bottom players on the pyramid beside his position. Of course the top player of lower pyramids also challenges horizontally. The object of this tournament is to become top man—"King"—and remain there.

This tournament is devised to accommodate decreasing numbers of players of superior ability, thus leading to a central position which is that of the champion. (See Figure 4).

Chinese Ladder

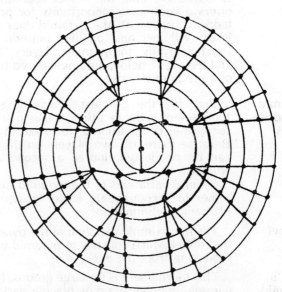

FIGURE 4. Chinese Ladder Tournament
A variation of the King's Tournament

This tournament, sometimes called the Spider Web, is generally used on playgrounds where a large number of participants are involved. It is best constructed by using round tags for name tags and hanging them on single hooks. Generally, each internal pyramid is marked with different colored lines, with the center three concentric gold circles as in an archery target's bull's eye.

In the Spider Web shown in Figure 4, each pyramid has 13 players and the eight pyramids join to four positions which in turn join to two and then to one. Players may challenge any one in the row above them in their own pyramid and, they may challenge any player in the same row in an adjacent pyramid.

Skyscraper

While this tournament is a self-perpetuation challenge tournament set up as a pyramid, it is also a type of elimination tournament. It is an excellent tournament for practice as well as for determining high levels of skill.

This type of tournament is best used where there are not too many players and it is desirable to spread the playing time over a considerable period. Ten to fifteen players make an ideal size group for this type of tournament. (See Figure 5.) There are only as many contestants as there are spaces in the lower row.

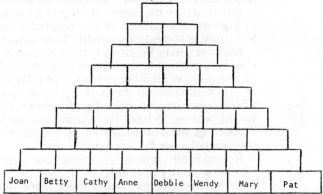

FIGURE 5. Skyscraper Tournament

Enter each player's name on the lower row of squares, one player to each square. No names are entered on the upper rows until games have been played and winners determined. In order for a player to advance, he may challenge anyone else on the same level he is on; if he wins, he moves up to the next level. Players may challenge only those on the same level as themselves. Players are eliminated when they become the last one left on a level. As there is one less square on each level, one player is eliminated on each level.

The number of levels for a tournament will be determined by the number of participants. There will be the same number of levels as there are players. This is an excellent tournament to use when introducing young players to the psychology of elimination tournaments. A player is not eliminated until there is no one left on his level.

ROUND-ROBIN TOURNAMENTS

Where time and facilities permit, the round-robin tournament is preferable to all other types of tournaments, because it operates on the principle of every entry playing every other entry an equal number of times, the winner being the entry with the highest percentage of matches won.

In a single round-robin, a single cycle is held, with every entry meeting every other entry once; in a double round-robin, every entry meets every other entry twice; etc. The round-robin tournament thus is the ideal framework for an entire season of play, since with a large number of entries a single cycle may last an entire season and with a smaller number a series of cycles may be scheduled, to extend over the period desired.

Scheduling Factors

In drawing up a round-robin schedule, numbers should be used to indicate the various entries, because: (1) they offer the only quick and sure means of checking a schedule to see that no entry has been omitted and that each entry is slated to play the same number of games; (2) they show at a glance the pattern of the schedule; and (3) they are less cumbersome to work with than names.

Numbers may be drawn at random for the entries or may be assigned to them; it makes little difference, since all entries play all other entries. But if there is any danger of dissatisfaction on the part of entries over the order in which they may be paired with certain other entries, it would be wise to have them draw lots for their numbers.

Pairings may be indicated by the abbreviation vs., by the symbol x, or by a hyphen.

Round-robin schedules should be arranged with the following points in mind:
1. No two entries should meet more than once in any single cycle;
2. No entry should be scheduled to play at more frequent intervals than any other entry;
3. Wherever possible, and practicable, entries should be scheduled to play an equal number of times on the same day of the week and at the same hour, if the schedule is so arranged that each round of play is divided among different days of the week or among different hours of the day. This precludes any entry's blaming defeat on having been assigned all the "bad" days or hours;
4. Whenever more than one playing area is to be used for tournament play, all entries should be scheduled to play, as nearly as possible, the same number of times on each area.

There are some disadvantages of round-robin tournaments. More than one team may complete the tournament with a similar won and lost record. In such cases, extra matches must be scheduled or the ties be allowed to stand. Whether or not extra matches are played, the round-robin is a time-consuming tournament.

A problem which may arise in certain round-robin tournaments involves teams which are often absent or which drop out. In the former case, matches may be re-scheduled or the "no-shows" may have to forfeit. In the case of one drop-out, one team of opponents will find itself idle each round of the tournament. In case of two drop-outs, there will be two idle teams, but they can not play each other as part of the tournament since the schedule must be followed rigidly. The absences and drop-outs cause enough problems that round-robin tournaments should not be planned unless the director knows enthusiasm and participation will continue throughout the season. Team games are more adaptable to round-robin tournaments than individual-dual games because teams carry substitutes who may play for absent or injured members; only rarely is a game forfeited because of absences.

Scheduling The number of games needed to complete a tournament may be calculated by the formula: $\frac{N(N-1)}{2}$; N equals the number of teams competing. Hence, with eight teams competing it would require 28 games to complete a round-robin tournament as: $\frac{8(8-1)}{2}=\frac{56}{2}=28$ It can be seen that a round-robin tournament of more than eight teams would mean an extremely large number of games. Ten teams would require 45 games; 12 teams would require 66 games; and 15 teams would require 105 games!

Usually when there are more than eight teams, the participants are divided into leagues each of which would play a round-robin tournament. Thus if there were 15 entrants, three leagues of five teams each could be formed. Each league would, by the above formula, take ten games. The three winning teams could then play a round-robin which would require three games. This would make a total of 33 games instead of the original 105.

When teams are to be scheduled for a round-robin tournament, the pairing must be done carefully to ensure each team's participation at regular intervals and to prevent any two teams from meeting more than once. A popular system for pairing eight teams is shown in Figure 6. Team one is held in a constant clockwise direction at the completion of each round. This rotation continues until one more move would bring each team back to its original position. This system may be used for scheduling an even number of teams.

Figure 6. Round Robin Schedule for
Eight Teams [28 games]

Round 1	Round 2	Round 3	Round 4	Round 5	Round 6	Round 7
1 vs. 2	1 vs. 8	1 vs. 7	1 vs. 6	1 vs. 5	1 vs. 4	1 vs. 3
8 vs. 3	7 vs. 2	6 vs. 8	5 vs. 7	4 vs. 6	3 vs. 5	2 vs. 4
7 vs. 4	6 vs. 3	5 vs. 2	4 ys. 8	3 vs. 7	2 vs. 6	8 vs. 5
6 vs. 5	5 vs. 4	4 vs. 3	3 vs. 2	2 vs. 8	8 vs. 7	7 vs. 6

Note: When there is an even number of teams, there will be one less number of rounds than the number of teams.

For an uneven number of teams, it is necessary to schedule one team with a bye each round. Bye is a term used to designate that no match is scheduled. In this case, hold the bye constant and rotate the positions of all the teams. Each team will eventually receive one bye. See Figure 7.

It is recommended that the beginning tournament director practice scheduling tournaments with three, four, five, six, seven, and eight teams, so that this operation becomes simple to execute.

Figure 7. Round-Robin schedule for five teams [10 games]

Round 1	Round 2	Round 3	Round 4	Round 5
Bye - 1	Bye - 5	Bye - 4	Bye - 3	Bye - 2
5 vs. 2	4 vs. 1	3 vs. 5	2 vs. 4	1 vs. 3
4 vs. 3	3 vs. 2	2 vs. 1	1 vs. 5	5 vs. 5

Note: When there is an odd number of teams, there will be the same number of rounds as the number of teams.

The round-robin schedule for five teams (Figure 7) covers only the pairing of the contestants. To complete the schedule, either assign numbers to the contestants or replace the numbers with the names of the players or teams. If two rounds of the schedule are to be played, the contestant listed in the first or left hand column may be designated as the home team. If only one round is to be played, then the home and away part of scheduling must be worked out so that each team has as nearly as possible, the same number of games at home as away. Where there is an uneven number of teams, each will have the same number of games at home as away, but where there is an even number of contestants, half will have one more game at home than away, and half will have one more game away than at home.

TEAM ROUND-ROBIN TOURNAMENTS

There are occasions when two teams of several players each wish to compete in a round-robin tournament between the members of the two teams. For example, four, five, or six players might make up a tennis, handball, bowling, horseshoes or shuffleboard team which might wish to compete against another similar team. Each player would compete against every player of the opposing team. In each of the schedules in Figure 8 the numbers represent members from one team, while the letters represent the members of the second team. There are as many rounds as there are players on one team and as many games as the square of the number of players on one team. In designating the winners, the total wins and losses of all members of one team are calculated.

Figure 8. Team Round-Robin tournaments for two teams.

FOUR PLAYERS PER TEAM

Round 1	Round 2	Round 3	Round 4
1 - A	1 - B	1 - C	1 - D
2 - B	2 - C	2 - D	2 - A
3 - C	3 - D	3 - A	3 - B
4 - D	4 - A	4 - B	4 - C

(4 rounds, 16 games)

FIVE PLAYERS PER TEAM

Round 1	Round 2	Round 3	Round 4	Round 5
1 - A	1 - B	1 - C	1 - D	1 - E
2 - B	2 - C	2 - D	2 - E	2 - A
3 - C	3 - D	3 - E	3 - A	3 - B
4 - D	4 - E	4 - A	4 - B	4 - C
5 - E	5 - A	5 - B	5 - C	5 - D

(5 rounds, 25 games)

ELIMINATION TOURNAMENTS

Elimination tournaments are, as the name suggests, designed to eliminate players who have lost games until there is only one player remaining. It is obvious that such a tournament is intended for fairly skilled players to determine the most skilled. The major advantage of the elimination tournament is the fact that it is designed to give recognition to excellent playing ability and to eliminate mediocrity early in the competition. Other advantages include the relative ease in conducting the simple elimination.

A disadvantage is that unless the tournament is set up carefully, good players may be eliminated early, thus negating the major purpose of the tournament. There are several forms of elimination tournaments, each of which is designed to have progressively fewer players at each round.

Elimination tournaments are based upon the perfect powers of two, i.e., 4, 8, 16, 32, 64, 128, 256, etc. Where the number of entries is not equal to the perfect power of two, a system of byes is used in the first round, in order to bring the number of contestants in the second round to a perfect power of two.

This type of tournament is best used when a schedule must be completed quickly and there is a large number of teams and contestants. In the straight elimination type, the number of games necessary to complete the play-off will be one less than the number of teams or contestants entered; where consolation rounds are used in conjunction with the straight elimination tournament, then the number of games necessary will be approximately twice the number of contestants. The same will hold true for the double elimination type.

In setting up this type of tournament, as in other types, the date, time and place of ALL games on the schedule should be incorporated in the original chart; the names of the contestants would, of course, be filled in as the tournament progresses.

Seeding is the process whereby certain individuals or teams are conceded to be the most likely to advance to the final rounds of the tournament, and are placed in the schedule in such a way that they will not meet in the early rounds and thus eliminate each other. This method assures more interesting and closer competition in the final rounds of the tournament.

For example: if there were 32 teams or individuals in the tournament, and four were to be seeded, they would be placed in the 1st, 16th, 17th and 32nd positions of the first round schedule. If eight were to be seeded out of 32 entrants, then they would be placed in the 1st, 8th, 9th, 17th, 24th, 25th and 32nd positions.

All unseeded teams or contestants would be placed on the schedule either by a "Luck of the Draw" basis, or just spotted in arbitrarily. Where byes are necessary in the first round, the seeded contestants, as a general rule, do not play first round games. While it is possible to rate all of the entrants in a tournament of this type, it becomes a very unwieldy process when carried too far; eight contestants are the usual number to be seeded and works very well, regardless of the size of the entry list. (See Figure 9.)

Where only four contestants are seeded, place their names on lines 1, 16, 17, 32.

If eight contestants are to be seeded, then place their names on the lines 1, 8, 9, 16, 17, 24, 25, and 32.

If the contestants perform according to expectations, then where four teams or players have been seeded, they should meet in the semi-final round of the tournament, and if the eight seeded players or teams are not defeated by an unseeded team, they will meet in the quarter-final round.

Whenever possible, place the most likely winner on line one and the next most likely on line 32; the next two contestants would go on lines 16 and 17. This spread will give the best possibility of the two best contestants meeting in the final round.

Figure 9. Placing seeded contestants

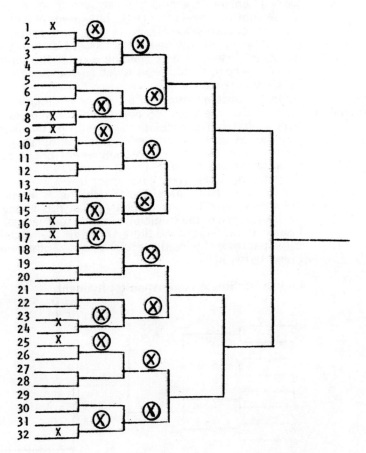

NOTE: X = A <u>seeded</u> contestant; Ⓧ = <u>anticipated</u> position
of seeded contestant in
2nd and 3rd rounds.

This illustration (Figure 9.) and the above numbers are true only for a bracket of 32. If a bracket of 64 were being used, the top four seeded contestants would be placed on lines 1, 32, 33 and 64, and the next four on lines 16, 17, 48, and 49 to obtain the same desired results.

When using brackets of 128 and 256, it is best to seed 16 and 32 teams respectively.

From Figure 9 it can be seen how it is possible for all of the seeded teams to meet in the third or quarter-final round in this 32 entry tournament.

Bye System   When the number of entries is not a perfect power of two, a plan is used that reduces the number to a perfect power of two for the second round. To find the number of bye's necessary, subtract the number of entries from the next highest perfect power of two. For example: if there were 43 entries, the next highest perfect power of two is 64, so subtract the 43 from 64. The answer of 21 gives the number of bye's necessary in the first round. These should be equally divided in the top and bottom halves of the schedules, and where seeding is used, the contestants who are seeded should be included among those who draw first round bye's.

Single Elimination One distinct advantage of the single elimination tournament is that there are no restrictions on the number of people that can participate. This type of tournament is also the easiest to administer. A single elimination tournament can be used for almost any event but it carries a definite advantage with larger numbers. This kind of tournament is relatively easy to set-up.

If a participant loses one match, he is immediately eliminated from the tournament—thus, this is one of the disadvantages of the single elimination tournament. If the loser is in the first round there are no further chance, but if the participant wins there may be many other matches. (See Figure 10.)

Figure 10. Single elimination tournament.

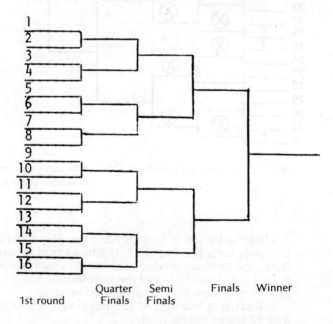

| | Quarter Finals | Semi Finals | Finals | Winner |
| 1st round | | | | |

Consolation Tourney Figure 11 shows how to set up a straight elimination type tournament with a consolation tournament for first round losers. This is a little better than the straight single elimination type, as each team plays at least two games before being eliminated.

As in other elimination tournaments, seeding is desirable for the most interest. Further interest may be added by having the winners of the losers' bracket play the winner of the winners' bracket.

In Figure 11, players A and P progressed to the finals where P became the winner. B, who was defeated by A in the first round, managed to win all subsequent matches on the consolation side.

Figure 11. Straight elimination tournament with consolation.

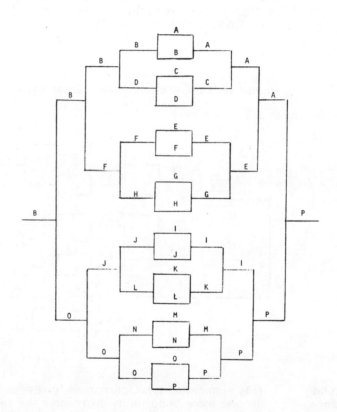

Double Elimination

Double elimination tournaments have become increasingly popular in recent years, particularly in sports such as baseball and softball.

Double elimination tournaments are best suited to 4, 8, 16, or 32 teams. In the event there is an odd number of entries, a team which draws a bye in the first round should not draw another bye after being relegated to the losers' bracket. Teams that have met in the opening round of play should not be paired in the losers' bracket.

Two defeats are necessary to eliminate a player or team. The losers in the first bracket move into the second bracket or losers' bracket. The players or teams that advance the farthest in each bracket meet each other for the championship. Should the winner of the second or losers' bracket defeat the winner of the first or winners' bracket, another game will be necessary in that each team or player must be defeated twice for elimination. The champion, possibly, may be the player or team that was forced to go into the second bracket the first round or thereafter.

The process of an eight-team double elimination tournament is shown in Figure 12. As each team loses its first game, it moves into the losers' division for further play. Another loss eliminates it.

Figure 12. Double elimination tournament.

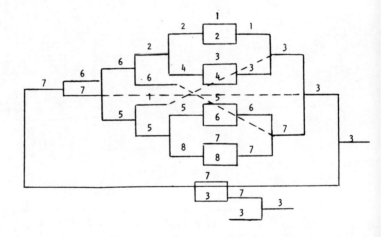

Second Chance

This elimination-type tournament gives each defeated team one more opportunity to reenter the play for the championship regardless of the round in which the team was defeated. In other words, until the final rounds, a team must lose two consecutive matches before it is eliminated from the competition.

The second chance tournament thus offers more participation than does the single elimination, but is more time consuming as a result.

The tournament chart for eight teams is shown in Figure 13. It should be noted that all teams do not play in every round. Byes are given whenever a team is awaiting an opponent and thus is not scheduled to play.

Figure 13. Second chance tournament.

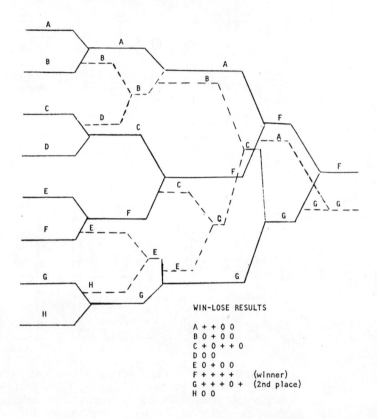

WIN-LOSE RESULTS

```
A + + 0 0
B 0 + 0 0
C + 0 + + 0
D 0 0
E 0 + 0 0
F + + + +      (winner)
G + + + 0 +    (2nd place)
H 0 0
```

MISCELLANEOUS TOURNAMENTS

There are several tournaments which do not fit into any of the three categories mentioned above; however, they are particularly useful in recreational settings such as playgrounds, drop-in hours, summer camps, and play-days.

Bridge Tourney

The bridge tournament is best where socialization is one objective of the total program of which this tournament is a part and where the tournament must be concluded in one day or a portion of one day. It is best for activities which are played for points, i.e. badminton, volleyball, cribbage, checkers, etc. It is an ideal tournament for a play-day. It should never be used if the selection of an uncontested winner is a serious object of the play.

In the bridge tournament, all contestants compete simultaneously, thus the number of teams is based upon the number of playing areas available. Figure 14 will help the reader to understand the mechanics of the bridge tournament.

Figure 14. Bridge Tournament

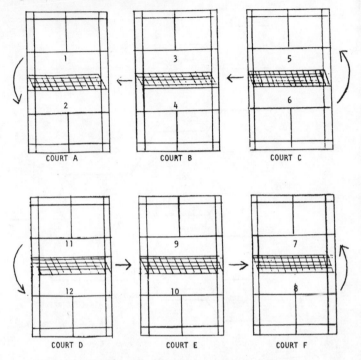

Assume that there are six courts, one hour playing time, and 12 teams of volleyball players. Team one is assigned to play team two on court A; teams three and four play on court B, and so on. Instead of playing for a given number of points, a bridge tournament is played for a designated period of time. For example, at the end of ten minutes, a whistle is blown. The team which is ahead at the time the signal is given is the winner of that round. The winning team moves counter clock-wise to the next court; the losers remain in place. At the end of six rounds, play is concluded. At that time the team which has won the greatest number of rounds is declared the winner. Or the team which has won the greatest number of points may be the winner.

A variation of the procedure is used when teams consist of two players as in tennis doubles or bridge. After the first round play, the winning team moves to the next court or table. Instead of the winners continuing as partners during the ensuing round, they separate, each one becoming a partner of one of the players still on that court. Winners of round two move to the next court and take new partners for the third round. Players thus have new partners during each round.

This bridge tournament variation is excellent for socializing purposes but is totally unsuitable for serious competition. The selection of a tournament winner obviously is difficult. This can be accomplished, however, in the following manner. A record of the number of each participant's wins may be recorded; this may be done informally by the players themselves. At the end of the playing time the person with the greatest number of wins is declared the champion. This tournament is popular at social recreation events where whist or bridge are played without serious competition.

Marker Tourney

A marker tournament is, in one way, a self-perpetuating tournament in that it requires no scheduling or constant supervision. It is a very informal type of tournament and serves as an excellent motivational device for practice. In a marker tournament, the goal is a pre-designated score, time or distance to be reached. When one individual or team achieves this objective the tournament is terminated.

Players may compete as individuals or as teams. When teams compete in activities with individual scores, the scores of all team members are accumulated into a team score. Archery scores, bicycling distance or speed, foul shooting, golf, horseshoes, swimming speed, self-testing skills and many simple skills all lend themselves to successful marker tournaments.

Examples of three types of marker tournaments are as follows: A group with the highest cumulative score in archery at the end of 16 rounds, which were shot at one round per day, four days per week for four weeks, is the winner of a timed marker tournament. A total score of 1000 is set in bowling; the first bowler to accumulate 1000 points is the winner. (This might be scheduled for one game per week until the score is reached.)

Swimming an accumulated number of laps of the pool during daily half-hour swims is a distance marker tournament. The first swimmer to accumulate a total of 100 laps during the scheduled hours would win. The first person to shoot 25 consecutive free throws might win another marker tournament, or the first person to do ten consecutive pull-ups might win another. There are innumerable possibilities for marker tournaments.

Ringer Tourney

A variation of the marker tournament is the ringer tournament which requires individual or team scores for an activity such as bowling, archery, golf, riflery, horseshoes, free throws and the like to be recorded, one or more times a week over a period of weeks. One way of determining the winner of a ringer tournament is simply to circle the highest score occurring during the predesignated number of meets. Another way is to circle each person's highest score each week and total them at the end of the pre-determined number of weeks. (i.e. If the groups compete three times a week, only the top scores are circled each week) Of course the person with the highest score would be the winner. This is another tournament which is an excellent motivational device. It is particularly good for beginners playing two or more games per week, for the poorest games are never included in the final accumulation of points.

Detour   One of the best practice tournaments is the detour. It is hard to understand why this is also one of the least used tournaments. It is particularly useful in a playground situation where a leader is trying to develop a tennis team, because each player has a chance to practice in each round where he is defeated.

This tournament exists for the purpose of providing extra practice for the less skillful teams. It is not an elimination type tournament, although it is charted in a somewhat similar manner. Each time a team loses a match it must detour, that is play a practice game before proceeding to the next round. Since a point is scored against a team for each loss, the winner is the team having accumulated the fewest number of points at the completion of the play. The detour tournament is suitable only for those numbers of teams which are a multiple of four (4, 8, 12, 16, 20, etc.), for the use of byes will destroy the order of play.

The charting of a detour tournament for eight teams is shown in Figure 15. The solid lines represent the rounds of the tournament, and the dotted lines represent the intervening practice matches. Losing teams are moved to the right for the practice game, but winners do not compete again until the next round. Teams must be rescheduled for each match since the design of the chart does not move teams automatically into correct positions.

In scheduling games, teams with no losses are pitted against each other in each successive round until only one undefeated team remains. At that point the tournament is ended. The round in which this occurs will be followed by the usual practice matches, after which the tournament is concluded.

Teams which have suffered defeats may draw or be assigned opponents for each ensuing practice game and round match. The assigning of opponents throughout the tournament has the advantage of preventing the same teams from meeting twice, in so far as this is possible.

At the close of round one, the losers play their practice matches. When these practice games are concluded, the losers' names are moved to the right to facilitate scoring. Round two is then scheduled. The winners from round one, teams A, C, E, and G are paired off and the rest of the teams again either draw or are assigned opponents.

Two more practice matches follow for the round two losers. The still undefeated teams, A and G, now meet each other in round three, the final round, and the other teams are paired off as usual. Two losers' detour matches complete the tournament.

Figure 15. Detour tournament.

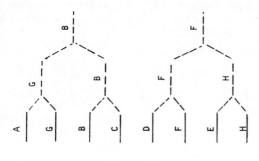
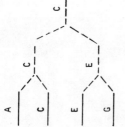
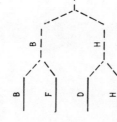
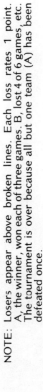
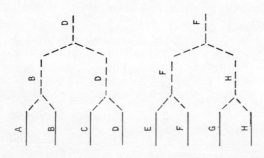

NOTE: Losers appear above broken lines. Each loss rates 1 point. A, the winner, won each of three games. B, lost 4 of 6 games, etc. The tournament is over because all but one team (A) has been defeated once.

Score (1 loss = 1 point)

A = 0
B = 4
C = 2
D = 2
E = 1
F = 4
G = 1
H = 4

18 Points (18 games)

Since each loss counts one point, team A wins the tourney with no losses and a score of zero. Teams E and G are second with one point each, teams C and D follow with two points each, and teams B, F, and H are last in rank with four points respectively.

"There are people who never make mistakes because they never try to do anything worthwhile."
—Goethe

Chapter 8
Social Recreation

It is a truism that people are gregarious. They wish to congregate in small or large groups to talk, laugh, observe or participate. Much of what people do in groups is actually a form of recreation for it is enjoyable, voluntary and done in leisure hours. Much of human socialization comes under the heading of social recreation.

Social recreation, by its simplest definition, is recreation which has socialization as its major motivating factor. This means that many recreational activities may be classified as social recreation even though their forms are entirely dissimilar. A list of activities which can be classified as social recreation includes parties, picnics, banquets, play days, campfires, conventions, class reunions and many other group oriented programs. Each of these activities relies on socialization for its success.

Parties generally include many types of activities including some which are competitive. Even though competitive activities may predominate, the socializing factor is of greater importance than is the winning factor. Simple skills, a few rules and improvised equipment are substituted for highly developed skills, exacting rules and precisely built equipment. Prizes may be nominal or non-existent and relaxation and fun for fun's sake take the place of a concerted effort to win.

Picnics undeniably are social recreation, for socialization is the motivator, not hunger. People who are hungry don't plan picnics or plan to attend picnics. They eat. People who plan to attend picnics really do so because a picnic is an ideal social event, not because they anticipate hunger. Eating together in an informal setting is fun. It is more work to prepare a picnic and pack everything up to take outdoors than it is to eat at home. Still, judging by the thousands of picnics held each year, the socialization is well worth the extra work.

By the same reasoning, eating in the more formal restaurants and attending banquets are activities motivated more by socialization than by hunger. A banquet is a lot of work, yet it is an ideal way for a group to celebrate a common cause as a group.

A play day, while consisting almost entirely of competitive activities, has getting together as its major purpose. A convention has educational objectives; yet it is through the socialization of the participants at and between educational sessions that the objectives are attained.

Another attribute of social recreation is that the events are of short duration with definite beginnings and endings. The entire event may last one hour, one day or a few days. Further analysis of social recreation shows that it is a program integrator. In other words, through the social program, the participants are integrated to think alike, feel enthusiasm toward a common point, and actually become, for a short while, an integrated unit. Like music, social recreation can transform a group of individuals into an individual group.

Both horizontal and vertical groups can have enjoyable activities through social events. A horizontal group is characterized by being a group which cuts across personal similarities. The Cub Scouts, or junior high girls, or the Grandmothers Bridge Club are each examples of horizontal groupings.

Vertical groupings are made up of many ages, interests, and abilities. Obviously a family reunion is a social event entailing a vertical group. Social recreation is probably the best form of recreation for use with vertical groups.

Because social events are adaptable to all people, a necessary attribute is the fact that not much skill, knowledge or preparation is needed by the participants. Even in a basically competitive play day or field day, there is little highly skilled practice prior to the event.

Equipment for social recreation may be simple, improvised or invented. If a picnic planning group wants to play horseshoes and can't locate any horseshoes, then bean bags, flat rocks, wooden blocks or even light weight pine cones may be substituted. A balloon may become a volleyball; a decorated grocery box may be used for a speaker's dais.

The characteristics of social recreation then are: socialization, short duration, group integration, horizontal or vertical groupings, little skill, knowledge or preparation on the part of the participant, and simple equipment.

PURPOSES AND VALUES OF SOCIAL EVENTS

The purposes of social recreation are basically the same for all social events, namely: getting people together for working together, playing together, learning together, being together, and having fun together. Depending upon the event, parts of this objective are emphasized or de-emphasized. The objectives of a conference are working, learning and having fun, while those of a birthday party for ten-year-olds are playing, learning and having fun.

Each person involved in a social event brings to it his own personal objectives and goals. The objectives of the leader, the participant and the sponsoring organization are usually somewhat different, yet they must be compatible. If a YMCA sponsors a one-afternoon camp reunion for boys who attended the youth camp last summer there will be three different objectives. The main purpose of the event as far as the sponsoring organization is concerned is to recruit campers for next summer. The objectives of the leader would include offering opportunities to renew acquaintances, offering safe and wholesome activities, reviewing camp skills and songs, and providing the participants with a good time. The participants probably attend the event to have fun and to do things with their camp friends. These objectives are very dissimilar yet compatible and logical.

The values of social recreation are primarily to the individual through the group process. This form of recreation provides opportunities for all the program participants to take part on an equal basis. Since skill and competition are of negligible importance, the unskilled can participate on equal bases with the skilled. The "skills" used in social events are usually those which have not been learned or practiced before and may never be used again. For those who are not competition oriented, there are many other social activities to participate in.

Another value of social recreation is the fact that group loyalty and solidarity and a feeling of belonging can develop through the social process. A municipal recreation department sponsoring a community Halloween party with special activities for all age groups can contribute to a feeling of community pride, loyalty, friendship and solidarity.

Certain social events can bring out latent talents in music, drama, committee organization, and countless other areas. Other social events, such as conventions, workshops or conferences usually are educational. Probably one of the finest forms of adult education is the conference or convention which one attends voluntarily for social, educational, professional and personal reasons.

THE SOCIAL ACTIVITIES PATTERN

Even though every social activity may be characterized by attributes which seemingly mask the socializing factor, the social events can all have one format or planning pattern.

The following outline can be used by anyone planning any social event. The outline is discussed in depth in the next few pages.

I. Background Material
   A. Type of activity, purpose
   B. Participants
   C. Date and time

        D. Theme
   II. Details
        A. Operations
           1. Facilities
           2. Promotion, publicity
           3. Decorations
           4. Refreshments
        B. Program
           1. First Comers
           2. Mixers
           3. Active events
           4. Quiet events
           5. Ending
        C. Financial
           1. Expense
           2. Income
  III. Follow-up
        A. Clean up
        B. Appreciation
        C. Evaluation
        D. Report

Basically, the Social Activities Pattern is the same whether it be for a small social party or for a convention for 2,000. The task is magnified for the convention but the organization includes similar consideration.

Background Material

Prior to planning the program of any activity of a social nature, it is imperative that background material be developed, for it is upon the background material that one bases the program.

Activity Type

Type of activity would include one of the following which, in part, designates some of the program components: banquet, campfire, carnival, conference, convention, fair, festival, field day, group trip, orientation, party, picnic, progressive party, reunion, talent night, workshop.

This list is by no means exhaustive as other events may be social recreation and follow the same pattern.

Purpose

Whether the purpose of a social event is simple or complex, the planner should be able to identify what he hopes will be accomplished through this event. The purpose of a banquet might be to recognize a retiring member, or to celebrate a victory, or to commemorate an anniversary. The purpose of a carnival might be to involve a wide range of abilities or a large number of participants. Or it might be to coordinate the programs of several playgrounds, to give recognition to youth achievement or even to raise money for a group through the efforts of the group.

If the planning committee can not identify the purpose of the event, it is questionable that the event should be conducted.

Participants

As in all other phases of recreation, the group is of paramount importance and, consequently, must be defined and understood before any planning occurs. In social recreation, because of the fact that the participants socialize and should develop a feeling of togetherness and compatibility, it is extremely important that the persons planning the event know as much as possible about the group in advance.

Knowing the age range of the participants is more important than knowing the ages of the majority. A family reunion with members ranging in age from six months to 90 years requires a different program than a class reunion with members ranging in age from 40 to 45.

It is well to keep in mind certain age traits particularly applicable to social events. Young children (ages 4 to 9) have short attention spans and a great amount of energy. They need more things to do than other age groups and must have things planned for them as they can not plan their own activities. They enjoy surprises and are generally in high spirits. Instructions must be given on their levels and the youngsters must be carefully supervised. In events where young children are part of a group with a wide age range, it is necessary to assign leaders to be with the younger children specifically and constantly. At this age, boys and girls will play well together but all need rewards, recognition or prizes (if there are any). It is a wise leader who plans calm activities to intersperse among the active ones.

Pre-teens in social situations may be awkward or blase unless separated from the young children for most of the activities. Boys and girls are better separated for some activities such as strenuous games or games requiring athletic prowess or physical contact. Other activities lend themselves well to coeducational participation.

Teen-agers can assume planning responsibilities for many social events. Committees serve the need to belong as well as to accomplish the planning. With careful supervision, teen-agers are capable of planning and executing dances, conferences, parties, work projects and many other social events. In cases where they can not be involved in much pre-planning, they can have responsibilities during the function. They also need an opportunity to be with their peers for socializing including much conversation.

Adults enjoy conversation more than any other socializer. The activity program should neither be crowded nor should it be empty. Certain recreational activities serve as ice-breakers and can lead to enjoyable conversations. Any adult social program, be it party, workshop, conference, picnic or whatever, needs a sound balance between structured activities and unstructured activities.

When social games are planned for adults, particularly older adults, certain precautions should be taken. Games or contests requiring blowing (i.e. balloons, ping pong balls, etc.) are definitely not for these people. Further, because of self-consciousness at being a lone participant, many activities whose rules call for individual performance, must be modified for group performance or for volunteers from within the group.

The members of a group participating in social activities may vary in physical and mental abilities. Planning for a veteran's hospital program requires a knowledge of age, physical condition and mental condition; the resulting plans should differ from those for a non-institutionalized group of veterans.

Other attributes of the group which must be taken into consideration in planning the program are: sex, number, educational background, socio-economic status, common interests, regional mores (dress, dance, drink, hours, etc.), marital status, purpose in attending, previous similar events.

Date/Time
It is self-evident that the time factor is an important planning item. The duration of the activity, however, should help determine program content. The types of groups and purpose of the event should help determine the length of the event. A holiday party for children should be about two and one-half hours long. A cookout or picnic might last five hours or more. Sometimes the duration of a program is determined by external factors such as cost, availability of a facility and continuity with other events.

There must be a definite starting and ending time for social events and a consideration given to the frequency of similar events. Some social events are scheduled on a weekly or monthly basis while others occur annually or, in the case of something like a fiftieth year celebration, once in a life-time.

Theme
Regardless of the scope of the program, every social event can be based on a theme and the use of a theme can enhance the success of the program. World Fairs and International Exhibitions are based on themes, as are national and local conventions. As a matter of fact, themes are used universally whenever a program is designed to develop a feeling of social-identity.

A theme is a single idea around which a program is planned. A party may be planned around friends from other lands, a circus, wild animal friends, pirates, hoboes, or countless other ideas. A conference training session or serious program generally has a more sophisticated theme such as challenge, progress, focus or relevance. The names of people of interest, such as Paul Revere, Stephen Foster, Daniel Boone, are used as focal points for specific fun days or festivals.

There are two major functions of program themes. One is that they help the participant to identify with a common idea. Because there is a known direction to the program, the participants are psychologically motivated to think along common lines. Through use of the theme the participants are unified.

The other major function of the theme is undeniably the fact that it helps make planning easier. The theme is the basis for decorations, invitations and sometimes refreshments. It helps set the stage or the general tone of the activity and helps coordinate each part. The theme helps the leader to plan the publicity, and to maintain continuity within the program.

Through proper use of a theme, participants can be in similar frames of mind before the first activity; it is a good theme which tells the participant in advance what to expect. Too often, when planning parties or programs, social leaders use themes which are too broad and tell too little. A party called "Christmas" or "Holiday Fun" or something equally broad tells us nothing. A Christmas program called "A Child Is Born" connotes a serious religious tone, as does "Joy To the World." "Christmas Capers" connotes an entirely different tone as would "Christmas Around the World," a "Christmas Carol Carnival" or "And All the Trimmin's."

Many activities held at Easter time are religious; yet many are not. A Theme "Easter" would mean a variety of things to a variety of people. "Life Eternal," "Spring Eternal," "Easter Bonnet Parade," or "Easter Egg-cite-ment" leave little doubt as to what type of Easter program could be expected.

Examples of various types of themes are as follows:

Parties:

A Hobby Fair
A Pioneer Party
The Year 2,000
Shipwreck
Rodeo
Kodak Kuties
Backward
A Prophecy Party (January)
Cupid's Carnival (February)
The Wind and the Rain (March)
Flanagan's Frolic (St. Patrick's Day)
Fool's Festival (April First)

Conventions:

The Challenge
Progress
Today
Focus
Beauty-The Fourth Dimension
Recreation: the Fourth R

Details

The details of the social activity pattern can be logically divided into three parts: operational, program and financial. The breakdown of each of these items is fundamentally the same either for short party or long conference; yet because of the wide variety in social events, there is much difference between the work of program planning for a two-hour party and that for a five-day convention.

Before planning the actual program, specific operational details must be worked out. Operational details are all those items which must be decided with the exception of

Facilities

the program itself. Generally they include facilities, promotion, decorations and refreshments.

After knowing the group, and before going further with any but basic planning, the facility where the event will take place must be identified, reserved and studied. The facility may vary from a room in a private home to a group of hotels and the civic auditorium in a convention city.

A facility checklist for special events follows:

Facility Check-List For Special Events

Facility_____

Reserved From_____

Open When_____ Keys From_____

Rest Rooms_____ Open_____

Fountains_____

Heat_____ Controls_____

Lights_____ Controls_____

Police_____

Fire_____

Equipment Available_____

Clean-Up_____

Trash_____

Parking Area_____ Number   Cost _____

Refreshments:

   Store_____

   Heat/Cool _____

   Serve _____

   Clean-Up _____

Promotion Publicity

Operational concerns include publicity which may either be a simple invitation or an elaborate series of announcements, articles and flyers. Invitations may be telephone calls, informal notes, catchy theme-oriented cards, or formal engraved notices. Publicity releases contain the same information but are intended to reach a greater number of people living at greater distances from the site of the function.

The purposes of publicity are both educational and motivational. Interest must be aroused in attending the function. Here careful selection of the theme may be a deciding factor. Somehow make the party sound glamorous. If personal invitations are mailed out, doing something different with paper, color, cut-out shapes, will be eye catching. For instance, invitations to a ''Sack Social'' could be written in crayon on very small paper bags. Invitations to a Mystery Party can be torn into pieces which have to be re-assembled to read the message.

If groups of people who are invited to attend a party are getting together at an earlier date, try putting on an impromptu skit. To advertise a ''Train Travel Party'' a small group could get together in a line, each holding on to the shoulder of the person ahead. One wears a high stovepipe hat and puffs a pipe to indicate the engine. Others have signs or costume props to indicate cars in the train; last comes ''the little red caboose.'' On the back of the ''caboose'' is a large placard inviting one and all to the party. The group goes through the meeting singing, ''The Little Red Caboose'' and should get much startled and hilarious attention.

At a dinner meeting preceding a ''Scarecrow Party'' a group could prepare a number of jigsaw puzzles ahead of time. As the guests arrive each can be given a piece of one of the puzzles. On the back is a number indicating their assigned table. When all were gathered for the meal, the puzzle containing an invitation to the party is put together at the table.

Decorations Decorations may be simple or elaborate. They may consist of flowers, centerpieces, streamers, colored lights, banners, costumes, etc. Decorations are generally in keeping with the theme and are used to set a stage or create a mood. They show that something special is happening and, like the theme, help the attendants develop a singular spirit.

Refresh-ments While it is not mandatory to serve refreshments, most social recreation leaders plan for them because they add to the socialization. They are looked forward to and, in most social events, refreshment time is a good change of pace from the activities. Refreshments may be as simple as coffee or soft drinks or may be as elaborate as a seven course dinner. In the party of short duration they are kept compatible with the theme. Usually refreshments tie in with the decorations as well.

Program Program details include all program events and their continuity as based on the theme. In planning the program for special events, one needs to realize that there is no single program format to follow since many combinations and arrangements of activities work well. There is, rather than a set format, a curve of action to remember. (See Figure 1.)

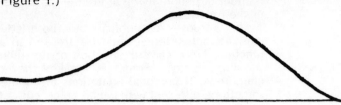

FIGURE 1. Social Action Curve

In social activities, the pitch of excitement is at a natural quiet or low level as the participants arrive and start "warming-up" to the activities and each other. The planner wants the group to leave the event calmly and quietly also, to assure a safe return home and to show consideration for the neighbors. This means that the leader plans that through the social events and the socialization, the high pitch of the event will be approximately mid-way in the time of the program. Refreshments are generally served about 2/3 of the way through the program and can serve as a quieting event.

In the case of a child's party, often a birthday celebration, refreshments are fairly noisy and are served just past the middle of the party. They should not be served last at a children's party for they are not calming.

The events after the refreshments should serve to completely taper off the excitement until at a definite ending activity, the party is over on a pleasant, peaceful note. This is hard to do with excitable children, yet a good story told after refreshments will often "do the trick."

While the order of events is not important, it is important that the party planned try to include: activities for the first-comers, ice-breakers, mixers, active events, quiet events and a definite ending so people will know definitely that the event is over.

Because first-comers arrive before everyone has assembled, they may find themselves at a loss for something to do. While they wait for the arrival of the last person, they need some activity.

First-Comers
First-comer activities are those activities designed for such people. A first-comer activity must be one which can be entered at anytime by one or more arrivers. It must last until after the last person arrives and takes part in it for a short time. It may be competitive or non-competitive; it may require group work or individual participation; it may

be a socializing, mixing activity, or it may be solitary; it probably should have written instructions; after it has ended, there should be a follow-up which gives recognition to many participants.

A good first-comer activity has a catchy introduction (related to the party theme), clear directions, and a definite ending which is controlled by the leader.

In many unstructured social events, the first-comer consists of hanging up the coats, being introduced to other people present, and being offered a cocktail or appetizer. In a structured social event, the first-comer activity is more of an active event with the participants actually doing something. Examples of first-comer activities are found in the Appendix.

Mixers   A social mixer is designed for the participants to move among each other and socialize. They must converse, question, answer or communicate with each other somehow. The purpose of the social mixer is to help people to get informally acquainted and to socialize with many others. Some mixers are also first-comer events. Examples of social mixers are found in the Appendix.

Ice-Breakers   Many times in social settings, reserved people are inhibited, or shy, or feel insecure. An ice-breaker or defroster activity is designed to break down social barriers through a social activity which causes some mutual amusement or mutual fun. Activities which help people feel at home with others generally involve all people doing something similar. First-comer activities which are of the mixer type are also ice-breaker activities. As the name suggests, ice-breaker activities help to thaw the frigid atmosphere which often permeates a group at the beginning of a party. Examples of Ice-Breakers are found in the Appendix.

Financial   While the finances of short-term social events are relatively simple, financing a major convention is quite complicated and entails a committee. The simple social event budget can be broken into the following classifications: invitations, decorations, equipment, prizes and favors, refreshments, rental (if any), transportation (if needed).

Follow-Up   There are four things which should be done by the leader before the job of administering the social event is over. First, the facility must be cleaned up, the decorations taken down, the equipment put away and the refreshment remains put away. Second, any persons who helped must be thanked. This goes for major social events as well as for small parties. A letter of appreciation is always in order to those who were volunteers as well as to those who were paid for their services. Third, even a short social event needs an evaluation. One simple check-sheet for rating a social event is seen in Figure 2. An example of an evaluation work sheet follows Figure 2.

Figure 2. Example of a check sheet for rating of social event.

SOCIAL ACTIVITIES EVALUATION
Check each item from 1 (low) to 5 (high)

ITEM   RATING

I. Planning
   1. Was activity organized?
   2. Was equipment readily available?
   3. Was there continuity and variety?

5	4	3	2	1

_____ Total

II. Program
   1. Use of theme
   2. Variety
   3. Movement from one activity
      to another
   4. Equipment
   5. Suitability of activities to group
   6. Beginning-First Comer Activities
   7. Ending

_____ Total

III. Leadership
   1. Enthusiastic and poised
   2. Prepared to explain activities
   3. Voice clear
   4. Position and posture correct
   5. Explanations clear and concise
   6. Mistakes handled tactfully
   7. Responsibilities shared
   8. Group control obvious
   9. Everyone included in activities
   10. Aware of group response

_____ Total

Final
_____ Total

Figure 3. Example of Social Recreation Questionnaire

EVALUATION OF SOCIAL RECREATION EVENTS
PLANNING

1. Is there definite evidence of careful planning?
   a. Was party organized?
   b. Was all equipment readily available?
   c. Was there continuity and variety?
   d. Did the party show unity, decorations, activities?
   e. Did the party rise to a peak?
   f. Was there a definite ending?
2. Were the leaders there well in advance of party starting time?

3. Was the party started on time?
4. Was the first comer planned for and made welcome?
5. Were activities suited to the group?
6. Did the leaders share responsibilities?
7. Were refreshments a chore, a bore, the peak or just another part of the evening's fun?

PROGRAM

1. Was there unity?
2. Did activities follow theme?
3. Was program varied in interest and activity?
4. Did events move smoothly from one event to another?
5. Was there time allowed for "breathers?"
6. Was there a climax?
7. Did guests know when the party was over?

LEADERSHIP

1. Was leader friendly and enthusiastic without losing poise?
2. Was he thoroughly versed in the activities he was explaining?
3. Were explanations clear and concise?
4. Did he stand where he could be seen and heard?
5. Was control of group evident?
6. Was leader aware of group reactions?
7. Were mistakes handled tactfully?
8. Was the leader a sharer?
9. Did he give everyone a chance to participate?
10. Was leadership responsibility shared?

Elements Nicely Handled:_____

Elements Poorly Handled:_____

A major event lasting one or more days should be evaluated on three levels: facilities, personnel, and program. Figure 3, obviously, requests an evaluation of program only. Many events have mediocre or at least less than desirable programs because of ill-prepared personnel or poor facilities. When these things are evaluated separately they give more information and help for planning the next event. The major purpose of evaluation is for planning another event. A second purpose, of course, is to help the leader to know whether or not his program was successful.

Personal parties, picnics and the like rarely require reports unless the leader keeps a diary. Special events conducted at youth camps, play-grounds, community centers, schools, youth agencies, etc. should have reports filed to help succeeding leaders plan succeeding programs. Any leader of a special event should probably keep copies of his reports to help him plan future events.

Summary   Social recreation encompasses any form of structured or unstructured event where socialization is the primary motivation. There are countless opportunities for persons working in face-to-face leadership positions to be involved in social events.

A leader is fairly much assured of a successful social event if he follows the Social Activities Pattern, making necessary modifications when needed.

*"A leader may affect
eternity; he can never
tell where his
influence stops."*
—Henry Brooks Adams
[adap.]

Chapter 9
Campfires

Flames
Licks of hunger in the air
Leaping high as if to snare
Creatures lying unprepared,
Shooting up in ribbons-keen.
Falling back to graves unseen;
Human viewers never cared—
Never cared for your short life.
Living in determined strife,
Circle round that wooden piece;
Choke its life with python skill;
Wrap yourself around until
Wooden strength begins to cease.
Melt its force until in death,
Sagging down with one last breath,
Leaving you to fade and cool.
Leaving you in pain to glow,
Writhing ebbing, dying slow,
Naught is left but one grey pool.

A campfire seems to have a magnetic appeal. People like to sit around a fire and talk, sing, or just watch the flames dance. A campfire lends itself to the development of a feeling of fellowship and companionship. Campfire programs have a certain mystical dramatic appeal and hold a special lure for the imaginations of young and old alike.

There are two basic forms of campfire programs for recreation: informal and structured. The success of both depends upon the same four ingredients interacting to create an image on the mind of the participant. The fire itself is the prime element; the people sitting around it, of course, is the second. Beyond these necessary ingredients, the program of activities and the ability of the program leader combine to determine the ultimate success of the campfire.

Campfire programs are best held out-of-doors with the participants sitting on logs around a fire. A campfire circle creates a greater unity among a group than does an amphitheater-stage type of set-up. The presence of other people on the opposite side of the fire helps to bring the group together and develops a feeling of oneness. The informal campfire program is best held for fewer than 40 persons but for not less than eight or ten. Fewer than eight means less comradeship, weaker singing, less group solidarity. More than 30 is unwieldy and hard to fit around a small circle.

The structured or ceremonial campfire can serve over 100 youngsters if well planned. The campfire may be in the center of several concentric circles of elevated logs. It may be elevated on a stage in a natural amphitheater. This writer prefers to use a campfire area which is a series of concentric circles broken to allow entrance and exit of participants and performers.

THE FIRE

The campfire itself is the psychological element which is the main focus of a campfire program. Regardless of what else is going on, the participant's focus returns again and again to the fire. A good campfire lights quickly, burns brightly, lasts as long as the program and glows beautifully as it dies down. The program itself should follow the spirit and intensity of the flame. The program should follow the same pattern as the fire—bright and noisy early, and calm and peaceful at the end. A campfire excitement diagram resembles the social activity curve in Chapter VII.

As far as the fire itself is concerned, to have a successful campfire, it is necessary to build one or more practice fires and time their burning. Different woods are available in different parts of the country, and each burns with a different speed and intensity. Certain woods such as cedar and pine burn rapidly, send out sparks and die down fast. Hemlock is harder to start, crackles loudly and leaves few coals. Green aspen smokes and sputters. Hardwoods such as oaks and hickories take a long time to start, burn with a lower flame than evergreens, last a long time, and make beautiful coals. Consequently a campfire builder must learn about the wood available to him and practice his fire.

A campfire should start rapidly without much smoke or a slow flame. Only an adequate supply of rapidly combustible tinder and small kindling will make this possible. The neophyte will use far too little tinder and the fire may not get going brightly until well after the program has started. The campfire should ignite instantly and stay burning brightly for about 20 minutes. Then it should die down to glowing coals in another 20 minutes. Generally it should not be necessary to add wood to the fire during the entire program. The fire, once ignited, should burst into flame, burn the wood, die down and glow peacefully without any human effort expended past the first match.

Because of doubt and insecurity, many beginners feel compelled to use kerosene soaked logs or some artificial lighting fluid to assure the immediate success of the fire. This artificiality is a sign of incompetence and leaves a tell-tale odor which gives the fire-builder away every time. The apprehensive fire builder would be better off using large quantities of dried wood shavings (or even crumpled and hidden newspaper). Only through practice can the fire-builder be sure his final product will work!

At every campfire there should be a pail of water and a shovel. A burlap sack soaking in the pail will make an excellent fire extinguisher if laid on flames which start from sparks flying into areas outside the fire circle.

THE PARTICIPANTS

The participants at a campfire may or may not know each other. But they will soon feel an affinity for each other though through the universal focus on the flame. In order to develop a oneness and not break a spell, it is generally desirable to set some behavioral limits on the participants. When this is introduced in the form of campfire traditions it becomes desired behavior, not forced discipline. Actually, much disrupting or disturbing behavior which breaks into a patterned campfire is created by those who have learned no alternate action.

In youth camp or playground campfires, there are several "traditions" which help to develop the campfire image.

How To Enter
There should be one specific area designated as the entrance and exit. In the broken circle campfire noted, the participants generally enter to the left and walk clock-wise around in front of the row of logs on which they are to sit, taking the vacant log furthest from the entrance. When leaving, the last person in is the first person out as the orderly process is reversed. Of course it really is immaterial whether the entire group goes to the left or to the right; however, it may be important that no one cross between one end of the opening and the other. Often there are wires for lighting the fire "by magic," props, or special markings in that area and if participants honor a tradition which prohibits crossing the opening, no one will inadvertently destroy a valuable part of the forthcoming program.

Hand Signal
The Indian hand signal for quiet (explained in Chapter III) is ideal for a campfire program. A leader standing hand-raised and serious-faced can calm a group down for the beginning of the program with less effort and more ceremony than one who whistles or shouts. This hand signal can be used throughout the program whenever it is necessary to move from one noisy audience participation activity to another. Like any other attention-getting device, however, it should be used sparingly.

Fire-Tending

In a small group campfire, youngsters often feel inclined to play with the fire. They move sticks and add sticks. Then there are always those who poke long sticks into the fire until the ends glow and then wave the end around, watching the pattern of the glowing coal in the darkness until it is extinguished. While fascinating, this is dangerous, for the flowing end may break off and light on someone's hair, on someone's skin or clothing, or more often, in a pile of dry leaves or tinder where it may remain unnoticed until a blazing fire appears. Children (and adults) should be cautioned not to remove glowing sticks from the fire. They might also be cautioned not to move any of the pieces of fire wood unless they are the designated "fire-tender."

In a ceremonial campfire, the fire, as stated earlier, should not need additional wood, but should burn down as the program elapses. There may need to be a fire-tender, however, to rearrange logs, to replace one which has rolled off, or to move some to the side if the fire is not burning down as it should.

Flashlights

Generally a campfire program begins at dusk and ends when it is so dark that the attendants' way home must be lighted by the flashlights they bring with them. But the flashlights can be extremely distracting if the attendants are permitted to flash them on and off during the program. A campfire tradition which permits no use of flashlights during the program is highly recommended. If the participants are requested to put the flashlights on the ground and leave them alone, they are generally cooperative. A few reminders and some group pressure generally serve adequately.

Applause

Good manners relative to applause and disapproval should prevail. Sometimes, particularly at Indian theme campfires, applause is replaced by a chant of "How how how how" or "Ho ho ho ho." Disapproval may be expressed by "Wah Wah Wah" or "Neechee, Neechee, Neechee" and the group can have a lot of fun using these vocal expressions. While cheers and applause are fitting and proper for winners of competition, it is unnecessary and actually bad taste for a group to applaud after it has sung. The song was a group effort, sung for the sake of singing, and for the group to applaud afterwards detracts from the activity itself.

Some skits and stories may be cheered or applauded but the legends, stories, poems or monologues given toward the quiet ending of the campfire should never have their mystical spells broken by sounds of approval. The thoughtful perceptive silence which follows a well-told legend or story is the most rewarding applause a story teller can receive.

How To Leave

As stated earlier, a campfire program, like the fire itself, should have a quiet ending. Generally the campfire marks the end of a busy day and the attendants proceed to bed directly from the council ring. Since this is the case, the beautiful peaceful mood of the termination of the campfire should prevail even until the last person has left the circle. The singing of taps followed by a silent retreat, the humming of the last song as the campers file out, or the sound of a camper chorus singing in the background while others file out all contribute to maintaining the silence. Many council rings have a secluded path lighted by lantern or flashlight leading to and from them. Campers holding torches or lights along the way also perpetuate the mood of serenity.

THE LEADER

The campfire leader himself must be able to follow the flame's pitch and modulate his voice and enthusiasm so he is loud when the fire is noisy and calm when the coals glow. He needs to be able to hold the attention of the group, yet allow the fire to hold their attention too. He must be able to control the group so that they too feel akin to the tempo of the fire.

THE PROGRAM

The program for the informal, small-group campfire is generally unstructured and consists of some seated games or contests, some stories and some songs. Often there is conversation, discussion, group interaction and a spontaneous program. A wise leader will have some program ideas in mind and will have worked with a group of campers prior to the campfire so that they will have something in mind.

The program for a structured or ceremonial campfire is much more elaborate, takes a long time to plan, and should involve a committee or a planning group. Every ceremonial or formal campfire can be based around a theme or central idea. Every activity can be modified somehow to bring themal continuity to the program, so that it is a complete package, not a series of unrelated incidents.

There are four distinct components to a campfire program and every campfire planner must take all four into consideration or there is no campfire program.

The Call   No one will know there is a campfire unless he is told. If the campfire is scheduled for every Friday at 8:00 p.m., no one will know the theme unless told. One way to develop interest in the campfire, to arouse curiosity and to initiate a mind-set toward a particular theme is through the pre-campfire publicity. This may be through songs, letters, announcements, skits, placards or a combination of methods. Attendants should learn of the theme, special events, the time, what to bring, what to wear (mosquito lotion might be mentioned in some circumstances) how to enter the council ring and perhaps some group assignments such as "Bring your group's best teller of tall tales" or "Practice singing 'Han Ska Leve" or "Have someone ready to do some magic" or "Challenges will be accepted."

The time for the campfire may be announced by bell, bugle, drum, or a runner at each unit. The planning committee can think of many ways of publicizing the event, announcing its time and leading the campers to the council ring.

Lighting the Fire

One of the major decisions in a campfire program revolves around how and when the fire should be ignited. The fire may be blazing as the audience enters; it may be ignited when the last member has arrived; or it may be started after the program has started and some introductory announcements are given and some songs sung.

If the fire is to be already burning when the audience arrives, it is more effective, if it is already nearly dark out, for a bright fire in broad daylight has far less magnetism than one which is the principal source of light. Many times the fire is ignited later in the program for no other reason than the abundant amount of daylight in the early moments of the program.

If the fire is to be started after the participants arrive at the council ring it is generally started with some ceremony and dramatics. The fire may be started by a person kneeling and using a match. If may be started by several people touching blazing torches to the firewood. It may be mysteriously started through no visible means. Several common methods are:

1. A single match;
2. Four torches representing north, south, east and west;
3. A candle burning under a can which is pulled away by a hidden string to allow the flame to hit the tinder;
4. A vial of sulphuric acid tipped by a hidden wire onto a plate of potassium chloride and sugar. (2 tablespoons of potassium chloride mixed with 2 tablespoons of granulated sugar. A 1½ ounce vial of concentrated sulphuric acid.)
5. A burning snake (of paraffin soaked gauze wrapped around a piece of ½'' manila rope) wringling into the firewood (as pulled by a hidden wire on a pulley.)

The important thing in the fire-lighting ceremony is that all readings, sayings, chants or responses must be done clearly and with a great deal of dramatic dignity. The following reading is dull when read without dramatic feeling.

SPIRIT OF CAMPFIRE

I am the spirit of the Campfire. I hide myself in the limbs and stumps of trees. I come not forth until you set me free, with the glowing match. I crackle and dance before you; I cook your food for you when you are hungry; dry you when you are wet with storms; warm you when you are chilled; protect you as you sleep; become the center of mirth as you crowd around me for song and story.

I, the Spirit of the Campfire, bid you welcome.

When a deep voiced camper, hidden from view, says this slowly, with dignity and force, as someone else touches a match to the tinder, it can be impressive.

Campers can also write their own campfire openings, endings or program inserts. The following was written by a college student studying to be a camp counselor.

The First Campfire

In the darkness of this circle we cannot see one another, and we are practically strangers. When we light this fire, even the small light of the match gives us some idea of those around us. As the fire grows we can see each other more clearly, until we can even make out the faces of those across the circle from us. Our week at camp will be similar to the lighting of this fire. We start out as strangers, but as the week goes by, and as we work, play, and worship together, we will know more people. The faces will no longer be dim forms, but will be the clear faces of our friends.

Charla Royston — University of Oregon.

The writings of Joan Anglund Walsh, and Gwen Frostic make beautiful campfire thoughts. If the person doing the narrative can be seen by the audience (or his flashlight seen through the shrubbery) he should always speak from the heart and mind — not from the written page. If he is so lazy that he can not learn his part then it appears that the part is unimportant. A campfire speaker must play his role as completely as the finest actor on a stage.

Because there are books on campfire beginnings and because leaders and groups must have initiative and develop their own lighting ceremonies, this chapter will not be devoted to samples of successful openings. To do so would only repeat those already printed.

Program Body No two campfires should be alike; yet all campfires can have programs made of all of the same ingredients or of some similar ingredients.

There is a place in a campfire body for: announcements, challenges, stories, legends, skits, songs, magical demonstrations and games or contests. Seated relays (passing objects), scavenger hunts for articles within a team (judged for quality, never speed), audience participation stories, action songs, Shouting Proverbs, and Rapid Fire-Drama are all easily adapted to the council ring setting. (E. O. Harbin: "The Fun Encyclopedia, Abingdon Press, NY).

The entire program from entrance to exit should not

take over 60 minutes with 45 probably being a good goal. Songs should be taught and practiced before the program so that no time is lost through learning new songs.

Ending The way in which the campfire ends is related to the way it begins. Each should be distinct, clear and purposeful. The campfire ending should be preceded by some quiet song or story. Then a poem, thought, quiet meditation and a last song serve as the curtain on the act.

Appendix

SOCIAL FIRSTCOMER EXAMPLE #1
Search Me

1. For each of the following descriptions, find one person who fits it. (Just walk around asking people questions.)

2. When you find a person who fits the description, introduce yourself, then ask him to sign his name on the line beside the phrase that fits him.

3. Do not use any name more than once.

4. When the instructor starts writing on the blackboard, find a chair and be seated at once.

5. Save this paper.

Description   Name

1. A blonde_____

2. Someone wearing glasses_____

3. Someone wearing a blue skirt_____

4. A veteran_____

5. A native Iowan_____

6. Someone wearing loafers_____

7. Someone born east of the Mississippi_____

8. A left-handed fellow_____

9. A girl wearing nail polish_____

10. Someone wearing white sox_____

11. Someone over 6 feet tall_____

12. Someone wearing a green sweater_____

13. Someone with a Bulova watch on_____

14. A person born in June_____

15. Someone over 21_____

       skier_____

SOCIAL FIRSTCOMER EXAMPLE #2

Welcome to our sports and games night. Let's get acquainted!

1. On the line on the bottom part of this sheet, write your name, tear the sheet in two, pin the bottom part on you.

2. Go around the room and try to unscramble the games and sports written on the tags of the others. Do not tell anyone what yours is. Let him figure it out for himself.

3. When you unscramble a word, write it correctly on the back of the top part of your sheet and add the name of the person who was wearing that sport or game.

4. When the lights flash off and on, be seated.

Your name _____

Scrambled sport or game _____

sellbaba (baseball)
flog (golf)
gnipgnop (ping pong)
taboollf (football)
coscre (soccer)
cheyko (hockey)
sedlurh (hurdles)
misgniwm (swimming)
tasnkig (skating)
rhyrace (archery)
lablandh (handball)

ennacigo (canoeing)
iksing (skiing)
notgoab (boating)
kiingh (hiking)
grideb (bridge)
repko (poker)
bascrelb (scrabble)
astanac (canasta)
shesc (chess)
shrececk (checkers)
loonpomy (monopoly)

SOCIAL FIRSTCOMER #3

Welcome to Our "High Society" Party!
Join the Fun—See How "Rich" You Can Become in a Few Minutes.

You have just received six beans each of which represents $100. The object of this activity is for you to collect more money (beans). You may collect one bean from each person you can get to say either "yes" or "no." Just ask questions. If someone answers your question with either "yes" or "no," he must give you one bean. Be careful YOU do not say "yes" or "no" or you must give away a bean to your questioner.
When the whistle blows, be seated and count your wealth.

SOCIAL FIRSTCOMER #4

Hi There: Tear this sheet in two. Write your name on the bottom half and under it draw (don't be too artistic) something to represent the title of a song. Pin that sheet on your chest. Now look at other people's drawings. Guess their song titles and write your guesses on the top half of this sheet along with their names. See how many song titles you can guess. You may ask all the questions you want—that can be answered "yes" or "no."

YOUR NAME _____

SONG TITLE PICTURE _____

SOCIAL MIXER #1

Human Bingo

Let's meet some new people!
On the signal to go, circulate throughout the room and collect
autographs. Get one autograph in each square. Do not use any person
more than once. When you have the squares filled in, be seated.
Always write your name so it is legible!

Your Name _____

SOCIAL MIXER #2 [ALSO USED AS A COUPLING DEVICE]

Round The Clock

It's TIME to get acquainted! Find 12 people, each of whom is like you in one of the following ways. Put your name on his sheet, his name on your sheet, beside the matching description. When you have all hours filled in, be seated.

NAME

1:00—Home is over 100 miles from yours_____

2:00—Same color hair as yours_____

3:00—Same color eyes as yours_____

4:00—Same initial as yours_____

5:00—Same color shoes as yours_____

6:00—Dislike same things_____

7:00—Same color shirt, blouse, sweater_____

8:00—Same color skirt or slacks_____

9:00—Like the same sports as you_____

10:00—Same marital status as you_____

11:00—Same size shoes as you_____

12:00—Same hobby_____

FIRSTCOMER IDEAS

The success of a party depends greatly upon a program which starts as soon as the people begin arriving. The evening may be made or marred in the first few minutes when the guests are assembling. The main purpose of first-comer activities, mixers, and ice-breakers are to get the people to mingle freely at once and to get them acquainted with each other. Particular caution should be used in choosing activities which will not be disrupted when others join.

First Impressions. As each guest arrives, a large sheet of colored paper is pinned on his back and he is given a pencil. He then approaches each of the other guests in turn, introduces himself and asks to have a first impression written on the paper on his back. He also writes what he thinks of the others on the paper they are wearing. After about ten minutes, the leader signals the end of the activity and each player reads aloud the "impressions" he has secured, that is, if he is not too self-conscious.

Mysterious Stranger. Announce that there is one person in the room who will give to the fifteenth person shaking hands with him a valuable gift. (And, of course, appoint the mystery man secretly ahead of time, and supply him with the gift to be awarded.)

Mystery Song. As guests arrive the name of some well-known song is pinned to each person's back. The players circulate, each one trying to discover the name of the song he wears by asking questions about it. Other players may answer only yes and no. When all have identified their songs each person must act out the title in pantomine and sing a verse of his song.

Blarney. As the guests enter, they are told by the leader that the first half hour of the party is to be devoted to finding out which of them has the best "line." Each is to pay a compliment to every person in the room—the more extravagant the better. The players take notes of the person paying them the nicest compliment and at the end of a half hour give that person's name to the leader. The champion "blarneyer" of the group should be given an appropriate prize—a can of applesauce for instance.

Back to Back. Partners stand back to back. At signal from leader they introduce themselves to the person behind them. When the whistle blows they quickly find a new partner with whom they stand back to back and to whom they eventually introduce themselves. Game continues until players are reasonably well acquainted.

Memory Circle. Players are in circle. One player says, "Good evening everybody, I am Mary Smith." Next player says, "Good evening, Mary Smith, I am Doris Brown." Next player says, "Good evening Mary Smith and Doris Brown, I am Ed Jones." Game continues with each player naming all of the other players who have introduced themselves before he tells his own name.

Chip and Chop. Players in circle. One player in middle points to someone and says, "Chip"- then starts counting to ten. The player pointed at must tell the name of the person on his right before the pointer gets to ten. Should he fail to do so, he replaces that player in the middle of the circle. If the pointer says "Chop"-player pointed at must tell the name of the person on his left.

Conversation Circle. Double circle. When music begins each circle moves to the right. When music stops, each player introduces him-

self to the person he is facing and discusses some topic previously announced by the leadeer (the weather, a movie seen recently, a book, a newspaper article read recently, etc.) Anyone without a partner moves to the middle of the circle where he will probably find one.
Get acquainted musical chairs. Players seated in a line. Alternate players facing opposite directions. When music begins the players stand and march counter clockwise around the whole line of chairs. When the music stops everyone tries to get a seat. (Leader has removed one chair so one person will be left without a chair.) Player without chair is not eliminated. Instead he introduces himself to the group, then sits in one of the chairs where he remains for the rest of the game. As the players march by him each one must speak to him, calling him by name each time he passes. At every pause in the music one more player is seated. Game continues as long as desired.

MIXERS AND ICEBREAKERS

Do your social affairs have that stilted, cold atmosphere? Are your social contacts limited to the other half of your "twosome"? Would you like to meet several people and see if they can influence you? Do you wonder how the other 90 percent of your guests look from up close? Then try some of these activities designed to help break down formality. If carefully planned and executed, these activities will contribute toward a feeling of fellowship and all-around friendliness. To avoid being "stuck" at your next social affair, plan to use some Mixers.
Human Lotto. Prepare a sheet of paper marked into 25 squares. (16-36) if smaller or larger group.) The squares should be at least one-half inch in size. Give each person a paper as he arrives and have him introduce himself to 25 people and get each name in one of his squares. When all squares are filled, have each person in turn read one name from his sheet. As a name is read, each person checks the square on his sheet in which the name appears. The first person to have a row checked out calls "lotto."
Double Handcuff. Cut strings about 36-40 inches long. Divide group into couples and handcuff the girl by tying an end of her string to each wrist. Then tie her partner's wrist with one end of his string, pass the other end through the loop offered by his partner, and then tie the end to his other wrist. The game is to get apart without breaking or untying the string. Looks difficult, but is easy.

Animal Name Cards. Have some colored construction paper on hand. As guests arrive, give them a 6"x6" piece of paper and have them tear out the figure of some animal. Place the name of the animal and use as a name tag. Each guest then makes a list of those present and attempts to identify their name tag animal.

Musical Chairs without Chairs. Men line up in straight line facing one way, one behind the other. Every other man places his left hand on hip, and the others place their right hands on their hips. Girls hook left hands in one protruding elbow and all face counterclockwise. Have one less fellow than girl. As the music starts, girls move around the circle and when music stops they must hook on to an arm—one girl to an arm.

Musical Chair Names. Losers sit. Others must call them by name before passing.

Magazine Treasure Hunt. Divide in groups of four. Place a stock of pictorial magazines on a centrally located stand. Provide paper, paste, scissors. Try the following hunts:
1. Find a letter. Clip as many forms or variations of the letter (leader choose one) and mount. Time 8-3 minutes.
2. Order your dinner. Make up a complete menu and mount on paper in order of service. Time - 3 minutes.
3. Tie Counter. Clip and mount on a sheet every type and kind of tie in the magazine. Double points for ties in color.
4. Spelling Bee. Turn to a page (leader select number) and select the most difficult word to spell you can find on the page. Clip the word and paste it on the sheet. Time - 1 minute.

Chinese Puzzle. Divide people into groups of at least 14 and no more than 20. Have each group form a circle holding hands firmly. A leader from each group is sent out of the room. The groups then begin to mix themselves up by moving under arms and around through their own groups without breaking hands. When the group is well mixed up, the leaders come back and attempt to unwind the group as rapidly as possible. The first leader done wins. (This activity provides many face to face contacts.)

Eye Color. As each guest enters, he is given four cards. These are headed "blue," "gray," "green," and "brown." On them are to be listed all the people present according to the color of their eyes.

Name Accoustics. Cards and pencils are given to guests as they arrive. They are told to print their full name in capitals vertically at extreme left. Then guests move about trying to find persons whose last names begin with the letters on his own card. No guest's name may be used more than once unless two people by the same name are present. (Might give two points for last names and one point for first names.) A prize may be given for the completed name based on longest name.

Circle Name Scramble. As players arrive, give each one a slip of paper and pin. Each player uses the paper as his name tag. Have players form a circle and face center. Have each one place his name tag on the floor in front of him with the name side down. The circle then moves to the left. On a signal, everyone stops, picks up the name tag in front of him and pins it on its owner. Repeat several times.

SPECIAL ACTIVITIES
Coupling Off Devices

So you want to pair your crowd off. Or do you want your people in groups? Here are a few fun devices that eliminate the time-worn, but painful, "Now everybody pick a partner." Some suggestions need preparation; some can be spontaneous; some will necessitate knowing your crowd; some will be good only for small parties. Use your ingenuity, adapt, or toss out, as you will.
1. **Clock dial.** As each person arrives, hand him a sheet of paper on which the face of a clock has been drawn. Ask him to obtain the signature of a member of the opposite sex next to each number on the clock dial. He must, in turn, write his name opposite the same number on that person's clock. Make it clear that people must exchange names for the same number. If A signs B's paper at

1 o'clock, then B must sign A's paper at 1 o'clock. You are now all set. During the evening, all you need to do is say "Look at your clock. It is now 1 o'clock; pick up your 1 o'clock date for the next game, dance or contest."

2. **Heartbreak.** If couples are desired, tear small hearts in two. Put half of each heart into separate boxes marked "male" and "female." Let each guest pick from the appropriate box and go in search of the other half of the torn heart. If groups are desired, tear large hearts into five or six pieces. Give a portion to each person. Then send him out to find the other portions of his heart.

3. **Cinderella.** All girls place one shoe in the center of the floor. At a given signal, the men rush to the pile of shoes, grab a shoe, and start trying it on successive girls, until they find a girl whose feet the shoe fits. Girls must conceal other shoe and can give no indication if Prince Charming is finding the right mate.

4. **Housewives Huddle.** Girls stand behind paper curtain, one hand extended through a hole in the curtain. Men choose partners from hands. (All rings must be removed.)

5. **Twin Musical Chairs.** Two aisles or games for the popular musical chairs are set up. In one game, all men are playing; in the other, all women take part. As people are eliminated singly in each game, they pair off. They chat or start some other contest until musical chairs games are finished.

6. **Petshop.** Men and women are separated. Each girl decides on the name of a pet which she feels closely fits her personality. She informs her group of her decision. Each man now comes to the shop to choose a pet. He pairs off with the girl who has chosen the pet he names.

7. **Double Hoop.** Two concentric circles are formed, men on the outside, girls on the inside. Outside circle revolves in counter-clockwise directions; inside circle revolves in a clockwise direction. When music stops, men pair off with girl opposite them.

8. **Affinities.** Give each guest a slip of paper with half of an affinity. He must find the other half. Examples:

Bread and Butter
Sugar and Spice
Salt and Pepper

Or, find partners geared to a theme. Comic strip characters such as Daisy Mae and Lil' Abner; historical characters such as Romeo and Juliet. Or, list authors on one set of papers and titles of books on the papers for the opposite sex.

9. **Where are You?** If you know the guests well—
a. Give each girl an actual description of one of the fellows. Let her go and find him.
b. Collect baby pictures of the girls and let each fellow go to find his girl by the picture given him.

10. **Song Titles.** Give each person a paper on which is written the name of a song. Ask that he conceal his paper. If six groups are desired, then alternate six titles of songs. When all have a song title, ask them to start moving around the room humming their song. When they hear someone else humming the same song, join them and keep going until all six groups have been formed.

11. **Card Decks.** Use two decks of cards in two baskets, one for girls, one for fellows. Each boy finds the girl who has the duplicate of his card; a ten of spades from one deck with a ten of spades from the other, etc.

12. **Blind date.** The girls are numbered. The boys are told how far the numbers range. A boy steps up to the door and knocks the number of times he desires. The girl bearing the number corresponding to his knocks will answer the door to meet her blind date. The two can proceed to another room for another game, refreshments, etc.

13. **Whistle groups.** As the crowd mills about, a whistle or chord is sounded two or more times. The crowd assembles in small groups the size of the number of blasts. Thus three blasts, three people in a group. If you desire groups two for couple games or eight for group games you can secure them by this method. Let the crowd form several different sizes of groups before signaling the desired size.

SUGGESTIONS FOR ROTATING PARTY GAMES
FOR SMALL GROUPS [20-50]

A. Organization
1. Keep teams small (4 to 6).
2. Limit time at each station so that all teams will get to all events.
3. Place stations (if possible) so teams move continuously in same direction (clockwise or counter-clockwise).
4. Give score sheets to leader with the schedule of stations as team is to progress. See that leader has a pencil.
5. Have leader write names of team members on sheet in order in which they are to participate.
6. Eight events are usually sufficient for any one party.
7. Write rules for each event on a card and thumb tack it on wall or floor or in a prominent place.
8. Have all equipment ready.
9. Number all events so that numbers are easily seen.

B. Conducting the events
1. Ask leaders to read rules as soon as team arrives at event. Explain rules to team.
2. Blow a whistle to start each playing period. All activities should start and end together.
3. At end of playing time blow a whistle and let each player finish the turn started before whistle was blown.
4. Record raw scores of each contestant and add up individual scores to get team score for each event. (It may be advisable to award team points for winning events as: 5 points for 1st; 4 points for 2nd; 3 points for 3rd, etc.)
5. Supervise events to see that rules are understood and observed.

C. General suggestions
Many of these games can be changed to become events for special occasions. They will be suggested below.

D. Suggestions for stations
Rules will not be given. They can easily be made to fit the age group and situation.
1. Quoit types of contests

    a. Targets may be a case of empty bottles; a chair turned upside down; candy canes or candles for Christmas parties; a wand held by another player; a board with hooks or nails; clothes pins clipped to the edge of a box or can.

    b. Quoits may be made of rope; jar rubbers; deck tennis rings; circles made from wire coat hangers; reed; embroidery hoops; tinsel twined around a heavy wire for Christmas parties.

    c. Decoys swimming in a tank or tub of water may also be used. To score, a ring must be thrown to encircle a duck's neck.

2. Target Pitching Contests

    a. Targets may be placed on floor, hung from wall or placed on tables or chairs.

    b. Targets may be calendars with large figures, muffin tins, egg cartons, waste paper baskets, corrugated boxes, jelly glasses, tin cans, milk bottles, hats, chalk drawn on floor or wall.

    c. The throwing object may be bottle tops, checkers, ping pong or rubber balls, peanuts, pennies, playing cards, clother pins, balls made from paper bags or stuffed cloth, bean bags, corn for Thanksgiving, popcorn for Christmas.

    d. Tossing pennies (or bottle tops) at floating saucers is also a challenging contest. Float saucers or pie tins in tub of water. Pennies must stay in saucer to score.

3. Bowling Types of Games

    a. Place golf tees in same formation as ten pins for bowling. Snap or push checker of bottle top to knock down pins. Score as for bowling.

    b. Roll a large ball at Indian clubs and attempt to knock them over.

    c. Roll a ball between Indian clubs and avoid knocking them over.

    d. Rolling a tire casing at Indian clubs.

    e. Suspend a hurl ball on a rope. Try to knock down Indian clubs on a return swing (ball is first swung forward and as it returns to player try to knock down clubs).

    f. Blow out candles. Set up lighted candles on table as if they were ten pins. Contestant places chin on edge of table and blows. Score as for bowling.

    g. Place a box or basket under the high end of a spring board. Roll a basketball down a lane and up the board to make ball fall into basket.

4. Miscellaneous Contests

    a. Funnel catch - hold a small rubber ball in right hand and funnel in left hand. Bounce ball on floor so it hits a wall. Catch ball in funnel (on fly or bounce).

    b. Hit the swinging bat - suspend a bat on a rope. Have rope swung from one side to other. Contestant tries to hit bat with a ball (basket, volley or soccer ball).

    c. Hit the clown - cut out a hole in a piece of cardboard (or corrugated box). Use soft balls made by stuffing pieces of old socks with rags. Have a person stick his head through the hole. Try to hit the ''clown.'' This is best played over a long table, target at one end, thrower at opposite end.

    d. Ring the bell - good for Christmas parties. Suspend a bell in a wreath and suspend wreath reach high. Use soft balls made from cotton or stuffed cloth. Try to ring bell by throwing at it.

e. Tire Target Throw - suspend a tire on a rope. Try to throw a ball through the tire while it is swung from side to side.

f. Shuffle board - draw a target on floor. Use tin can lids (from peanut or coffee cans) for disks and use wands for cues or slide disks with hands. For Halloween use brooms for cues.

g. Transfer ping pong balls from one place to anoher using a pancake turner. Do not hand balls with hands.

h. Cut out large jigsaw puzzles. Let group put them together. Score either by time or number of pieces completed.

Special Halloween Contests

1. Draw a target and in each section write a fortune (example: Great Wealth). Throw, slide or push bean bags or can lids into the target.

2. Try to ring the witch's broomstick (form of quoits).

3. Draw a large jack-o-lantern and cut out holes for eyes, nose or use a real pumpkin jack-o-lantern. Toss objects like corn into the target.

Special Christmas Contests

1. See how many words a group can write using the letters in the word Christmas. Score 1 point for each word.

2. Have group draw and decorate a Christmas tree. Judges award places for scoring points.

3. Draw a picture of a sock or Santa's bag. Cut out a hole. Throw bean bags (or any similar articles) into hole to fill the sock (or bag).

4. Draw and cut out a variety of toys from cardboard or thin wood. Each toy must have a wire loop at top. Arrange toys on a rack of of some kind. With a fishing pole, line and hook (drapery hook or one made of wire) try to hook a toy. Give each contestant a limited amount of time.

5. Quoits using tinsel hoops and candles of candy canes.

SIMPLE EQUIPMENT GAMES

Card toss. Place a wastepaper basket, a large kettle or a box on the ground. From a line ten feet distant, toss playing cards or paper plates into the container. The players have three tries each turn and each successful effort scores one point.

Muffin pan coin toss. Provide a muffin pan and a penny, a nickle, a dime, a quarter and a half-dollar. Fit cardboard disks into each compartment of the pan and number the disks. Put the pan on the ground about five feet from the pan. Players take turns in trying to toss the coins into the pan and receive points determined by the number marked on the sections in which the coins remain.

Pie Plate Sailing. Throw pie plates or paper plates for distance or accuracy.

Rope Skip. Skip for endurance, fancy steps, etc. Recall childhood contests.

Bean Lift. Fill a bowl with dried beans. Lift beans into a saucer using two knitting needles. At the end of the playing period, note the number of beans successfully transferred.

Toothpicks and Bottles. Place an empty catsup bottle on a picnic table or tree stump, limiting teams to four or five players for each bottle. Use time limit; see how many toothpicks (or matches) they can successfully pile one at a time across the bottle opening without any of the toothpicks falling. When any fall, they must be replaced one at a time. (To play individually, the contestants take their turns one at a time. When a contestant, in the process of placing a stick, knocks off any other sticks, he must add those to his own personal pile. Object is to get all of your toothpicks on the bottle.)

Sack race. All contestants stand hip high in gunny sacks at the starting line. At the signal, they jump, run or walk as best they can to the finish line.

Three-Legged Race. Use a belt or cord and tie the inside ankles of two people together. Contestants race by couples to finish line.

Loose Caboose. Groups of three to six players. Each player in a group lines up behind one player who is the "engine," holding one another around the waist or arms. One or more extra players are left out of the formation. These are the "loose cabooses." They try to catch on to the end of the various "trains." When a "caboose" is successful, the "engine" of the group becomes a "loose caboose."

GUESSING CONTESTS

Guessing contests are always popular and can be used to keep early-comers busy. Articles should be on display in a prominent spot and paper and pencil securely fastened beside each for individuals to make notes of their answers.

Number of peanuts in a bag
Number of beans in a bottle
Number of apples in a basket
Number of kernels of corn on a cob

Weight of some well-known person present
Number of feet of string in a ball
Quantity of water in a can
Height of a specific tree

HORSENGOGGLE

The leader says, "One, two, three, Horsengoggle," shaking his clenched fist forward on each count. On "Horsengoggle," all participants hold up any desired fingers of one hand (0 to 5). The leader sums or counts all extended fingers and announces the total. He then starts counting and pointing to the participants in order until he reaches the designated sum. The person who receives that number wins.

SAMPLE OF ACTIVITY DIRECTIONS

Activity: **Calf Tying Relay**   **Type: Relay**

Equipment: 1 ball of soft twine or yarn per team.

Formation: Even Teams in single file relay (could be spoke, square or circle). Seated teams are best.

Directions: The first person in each line has a ball of twine. On the signal to go, the first person in each line ties a simple over-hand knot around one wrist, unrolls the twine so he can wrap it once around his waist and hands the twine to the next person who in turn wraps the twine completely around his waist, unrolling it as he proceeds. Continue to the last man who wraps the twine around his waist and then unwraps it and winds the twine up again. Each player in turn, unwraps himself and winds the twine up. When the leader finishes, he leaves the twine knotted around his wrist and holds the ball of twine over his head to signal he has finished.

Bibliography

Baird, Forrest, J. Music Skills for Recreation Leaders. Dubuque, IA: Wm. C. Brown Company, 1967.

Barsness, Linda Ann and Bischoff, Judith. Embers. (Song Book) Ankey, IA, North Polk Printers.

Berger, H. Jean. Program Activities for Camps. (Card File) Minneapolis, MN: Burgess Publishing Company, 1969.

Borst, Evelyn and Mitchell, Elmer. Social Games for Recreation (2nd ed). New York, NY: Ronald Press, 1959.

Boyd, Neva. Handbook of Recreational Games. New York, NY: Dover Publications, 1973.

Britten, Rodney M. and Bone, Maurice D. Leader's Guide to Christian Outdoor Education. Philadelphia, PA: United Church Press, 1971.

Buskin, David. Outdoor Games. New York, NY: The Lion Press, 1966.

Chase, Richard. American Folk Tales and Folk Songs. New York, NY: Dover Press, 1971.

Corbin, Dan H. Recreation Leadership (3rd ed). Englewood Cliffs, NJ: Prentice-Hall, 1970.

Eisenberg, Helen and Larry. Handbook of Skits and Games. New York, NY: Association Press, 1973.

Harbin, E. O. The Fun Encyclopedia. Nashville, TN: Abingdon Press.

Harris, Jane A. Dance a While (Rev Ed). Minneapolis, MN: Burgess Publishing Company, 1968.

Harris, Jane A. Dance a While (rev ed). Minneapolis, MN: Burgess Publishing Company, 1968.

Kohl, Marguerite and Young, Frederica. Games for Children. New York, NY: Cornerstone, 1971.

Kohl, Marguerite and Young, Frederica. Games for Grownups. New York, NY: Cornerstone, 1971.

Kraus, Richard, Recreation Leaders Handbook. New York, NY: McGraw-Hill Book Company, 1955.

Nagel, Myra, My Keys to Creative Ceremonies. Jacksonville, AK: My Books, 1975.

Mulac, Margaret E. Games and Stunts for Schools, Camps and Playgrounds. New York. NY: Harper and Row, 1964.

Nelson, Esther L. Dancing Games for Children of All Ages. New York, NY: Sterling, 1973.

Sing. (Song Book) Delaware OH: Cooperative Recreation Service, 1966.

Tent and Trail Songs, (Song Book) Delaware, OH: Cooperative Recreation Service, 1966.

Thurston, LaRue. Good Times Around the Campfire. New York, NY: Association Press, 1967.

Tobbitt, Janet. Counselor's Guide to Camp Singing. Martinsville, IN: American Camping Association, 1971.

Vick, Marie and Cox, Roseann McLaughlin. A Collection of Dances for Children. (Card File) Minneapolis, MN: Burgess Publishing Company, 1970.

Ward, Jane Shaw, Tajar Tales (rev). Martinsville, IN: American Camping Association. 1967.

Winslow, Barbara. Spotlight on Drama in Camp. Martinsville, IN: American Camping Association, 1962.

Woodsmoke and Campfire Hints. Martinsville, IN: American Camping Association, 1976.